DATE DUE

Demco, Inc. 38-293

HISTORICAL ROMAN COINS

HISTORICAL ROMAN COINS

By

G. F. HILL

Late Director and Principal
Librarian
Department of Coins and Medals
British Museum

FAIRFIELD UNIV. LIBRARY

DEC 1 8 1995

ARES PUBLISHERS INC.
CHICAGO   MCMLXXVI

Unchanged Reprint of the Edition:
London, 1909
ARES PUBLISHERS INC.
612 N. Michigan Avenue
Chicago, Illinois 60611
Printed in the United States of America
International Standard Book Number:
0-89005-065-1
Library of Congress Catalog Card Number:
76-6019

PREFACE

THIS volume is intended as a companion to *Historical Greek Coins*, published three years ago.

The evidence afforded by Roman coins as to the course of Roman history is of two kinds. The first, and the more valuable, is contemporary evidence; the historian has to extract from the extant coins such information as they provide concerning the circumstances in which they were cast or struck. But, owing to the commemorative habit, which was strong in the Roman race, a certain number of coins illustrate the history of a period which was past when they were issued. Such pieces give us evidence less trustworthy than the first kind, although not infrequently there is less opportunity of error in the interpretation of their meaning. But they are incidentally of interest as indicating the state of opinion which prevailed at the time when they were issued. A case in point is the coin, struck in the first century B.C., commemorating the mission of Lepidus to Egypt at the end of the third century. However, in the selection of coins for this volume, preference has naturally been given to pieces of the contemporary kind.

The dry, matter-of-fact temperament of the Romans

PREFACE

is naturally reflected in their coinage. The artist is seldom carried away by any flight of artistic imagination from his immediate purpose, which is to provide a convenient medium of exchange; his allegories and his symbolism tend to be crude and frigid; his references to events are, as far as possible, direct and pointed. One cannot imagine a Greek of the fifth or fourth century proclaiming to the world, with the help of an inscription, that his coins were issued "for the purchase of corn." As for artistic conception and execution, traces of good style are here and there faintly perceptible in the earliest coinage, where it was under Greek influence. Towards the end of the Republic the workmanship improves, and the coins provide a certain number of striking portraits. But even the best Greek engravers employed during the Augustan age seldom succeed in producing a reverse design that has any merit as a work of art.

In Roman numismatics, therefore, the pursuit of the truth is deprived of some of the attractions which the study of Greek coins presents. But there is no lack of sport, for anyone who is interested in the interpretation of obscure types, or in the reconciliation of confused or corrupt passages in Roman historians or antiquaries with the evidence of the coins.

Until recently the history of the earliest Roman coinage has been involved in the utmost obscurity. But the distinguished scholar and collector, Dr. E. J.

PREFACE

Haeberlin of Frankfurt, in the most remarkable contribution that has been made in recent years to any branch of numismatics, has thrown a flood of light on the subject, and shown how much in the coinage that has seemed unintelligible and chaotic is, when properly interpreted, a clear and orderly development, marching side by side with the progress of Rome as a power in Italy and in the ancient world.

In the period following the introduction of the *denarius*, the arrangement of the coinage presents problems of a different kind, soluble rather by minute and patient comparison and classification than by the exercise of the historical imagination. In this field the work that was done by Count J. F. W. de Salis, although almost unknown even to professional numismatists, is of extraordinary importance. The whole of the vast Roman and Byzantine collection in the British Museum was arranged by him in the light of his unrivalled knowledge and experience. Enormous quantities of coins, singly or in hoards, passed through the hands of this indefatigable collector, and his eye for fabric and style seems to have become almost infallible. The trays of the British Museum collection have long preserved, in their arrangement, almost the only record of his work; for he seems to have been singularly averse to publication. Of late, however, his services to Byzantine numismatics have been duly acknowledged by Mr. Wroth, in the Preface

PREFACE

to his *Catalogue of the Imperial Byzantine Coins in the British Museum*. And his still more important work on the Republican period will be embodied in the forthcoming British Museum *Catalogue of Roman Republican Coins*, by Mr. H. A. Grueber.

The fact that, by Mr. Grueber's kindness, I have been able during the preparation of this volume to consult the proof-sheets of his Catalogue, so far as it had advanced, has made my task very much less troublesome than it might have been. But this bald statement by no means expresses the amount of my debt to his unfailing kindness and readiness to place his knowledge at my disposal in difficult questions of arrangement and interpretation. References to the forthcoming Catalogue are, where possible, inserted after the descriptions of the coins.

Mr. George Macdonald also, with characteristic generosity, undertook to read not merely the proofs, but the even less attractive manuscript of the book. Those who know his published work need not be told that his criticisms have been invaluable.

I have also, as usual, to thank the authorities of the Berlin and Paris Cabinets, especially Dr. K. Regling, M. A. Dieudonné and M. J. de Foville, for kindly providing casts of certain coins not represented in the British Museum.

G. F. HILL.

January, 1909.

GLOSSARY

OF SOME TECHNICAL TERMS USED IN THE TEXT

Aes grave: the early heavy circular coinage of bronze of Rome and Italy. See p. 11.

Aes rude: the amorphous lumps of bronze used as currency in Italy before the introduction of coinage proper. See pp. 13, 14.

Aes signatum: a term applied to the large quadrilateral "bricks" issued by the Roman mint. See p. 13.

As: a bronze coin originally corresponding in weight to the *libra* or pound; afterwards reduced. See p. 6 and *passim*.

Attic Standard: *see* Euboic-Attic.

Aureus: a gold coin, usually equivalent to 25 denarii. See Nos. 51, 55, 56, 58, etc.

Bigatus: a coin of which the type is a two-horse chariot. See p. 60.

Blank: *see* Flan.

Campanian Standard: a standard derived from the Phoenician, the didrachm weighing 7·76 grammes (later reduced to 6·82 grammes).

Canting Type or **Symbol**: a type or symbol which indicates, by means of a pun, the person or state to which it refers, as the flamen's cap of Flamininus.

Cast Coins: *see* Struck.

Coin: a piece of metal (or, exceptionally, some other convenient material) artificially shaped and marked with a sign or type as a guarantee of its quality and weight, and issued by some responsible authority, to serve primarily as a medium of exchange, in terms of which the value of exchangeable commodities can be expressed. Distinguished from a token by having or being supposed to have an intrinsic value more or less nearly approaching the value imposed upon it by the issuing authority.

Countermark: a small mark impressed on a coin, usually by some person other than the issuing authority, and intended to give the coin fresh currency.

GLOSSARY

Denarius: a silver coin equivalent originally to 10, later to 16 *asses*. See pp. 29, 47 and *passim*.

Didrachm: piece of two drachms, q.v.

Die: the instrument containing the design which, by being impressed, produces the type on a coin. The coin in striking was placed between the upper and lower dies. The lower die in ancient times was usually let into an anvil, its fellow inserted in the lower end of a bar of metal, the other end of which could be struck with the hammer.

Drachm: a division of the stater (q.v.), usually one-half, but in some systems, as the Corinthian, one-third. Usually derived (after Plutarch *Lysand.* 17) from δράττεσθαι, as representing a "handful" of obols. This is probably a popular etymology, and *drachm* may be the same word as the Phoenician *darkemon*.

Dupondius: a coin of two *asses*. See Nos. 4, 98.

Electrum (ἤλεκτρον, λευκὸς χρυσός): any alloy, whether natural or artificial, of gold or silver, in which there is more than twenty per cent. of silver.

Euboic-Attic Standard: the standard based on a unit (stater) of 8·72 grammes. See Nos. 5, 6.

Exergue: that segment of the field of a coin which, lying below the type, is separated from the rest of the field either by the lower outline of the type itself, or by a line drawn expressly for the purpose.

Fabric: the external shape and appearance given to coins by the mechanism employed to cast or strike them; distinct therefore from style, which is conditioned by the artistic qualities of the designer.

Field: that portion of the surface of a coin (within the border, if any) which is not occupied by the type.

Flan or blank: the shaped piece of metal which is made into a coin by having the necessary types impressed on it.

Libella: $\frac{1}{10}$ *scripulum* in the Romano-Campanian system; a bronze coin nominally equivalent to $\frac{1}{10}$ *scripulum* of silver. See p. 22.

Litra: the Sicilian or Italian pound of copper or bronze; or the silver coin of 0·87 gramme which was originally the equivalent of the pound of copper; or the bronze token nominally representing the pound of copper. See No. 49.

GLOSSARY

Obverse: the side of a coin impressed by the lower die, which was let into an anvil. Since, when one of the two types of a coin was a human head, it was usually produced by the lower die, it has become usual to regard the side with the head, by whichever die it was produced, as the obverse.

Osco-Latin Standard: standard according to which the pound weighed 272·88 grammes. See p. 6.

Quadrans: one-fourth of an *as*, q.v.

Quadrigatus: a coin of which the type is a four-horse chariot. See p. 25.

Quinarius: a silver coin equivalent originally to 5 *asses*; half the *denarius*, q.v.

Reverse: the side of a coin impressed by the upper die: *see* Die.

Roman Standard: standard according to which the pound weighed 327·45 grammes. See p. 6.

Scripulum or **scruple**: $\frac{1}{288}$ of the Roman pound, *i.e.*, 1·137 grammes. See p. 17.

Semis: one-half of an *as*, q.v.

Semuncial Standard: standard according to which the *as* weighed normally half an *uncia*. See No. 54.

Serratus: a coin with notched edges. See No. 47.

Sestertius: (1) a silver coin originally equivalent to $2\frac{1}{2}$ *asses*, $\frac{1}{4}$ *denarius*, q.v.; (2) a brass coin introduced by Augustus, equivalent to 4 *asses*. See No. 97.

Sextans: one-sixth of an *as*, q.v.

Sextantal Standard: standard according to which the *as* weighed normally a *sextans* or two *unciae*. See p. 30.

Shekel: the name for the unit of weight in the Oriental coin-standards. *Cp.* Stater.

Standard: a system of weights according to which the various denominations of a coinage are fixed.

Stater: the standard or unit-coin in any system; *e.g.* the Attic silver stater was a tetradrachm of 17·44 grammes, the Attic gold stater a didrachm of 8·72 grammes, the Corinthian silver stater a tridrachm of 8·72 grammes. *Cp.* Shekel.

Struck Coins: coins on which the designs are produced by dies impressed on the previously fashioned blank by blows with a hammer; opposed to **cast** coins, which are produced by the single process of pouring molten metal into a mould.

GLOSSARY

Symbol: a subsidiary type, being either (1) an attribute of the chief type, as the eagle of Jupiter, or (2)—and this is the strict numismatic use of the term—independent of the chief type, and serving to identify a person (as the authority responsible for the issue of the coin) or a mint (where the chief types indicate not the place of issue but the ruler).

Tressis: a coin of three *asses*. See p. 12.
Triens: one-third of an *as*, q.v.
Triental Standard: standard according to which the *as* weighed normally a *triens* or four *unciae*. See p. 30.
Type: the design on a coin. In the narrower sense, the essential portion of the design (as distinct from adjunct, inscription, border, etc.), which is the distinguishing mark of the issuing authority and guarantee of the good quality of the coin. *Effigies est nummi qualitas extrinseca, et signum testimonii publici* (Jac. Lampadius, *de Natura Nummi*).

Uncia: one-twelfth of an *as*, q.v.
Uncial Standard: standard according to which the *as* weighed normally one *uncia*. See p. 47.

Victoriatus: a silver coin weighing originally 3 scruples (¾ *denarius*). See pp. 35 f., 44 f.

LIST OF THE CHIEF ABBREVIATIONS USED IN THE TEXT

Babelon = E. Babelon: *Monnaies de la République romaine*. Paris, 1885, 1886.

B.M.C. = British Museum Catalogue. Where no further title is given, the volumes are those of the Catalogue of Roman Republican Coins, by H. A. Grueber. Otherwise a word in italics, such as *Italy*, denotes the particular volume of the Catalogue of Greek Coins referred to.

Eph. Epigr. = *Ephemeris Epigraphica* (Berlin).

J.H.S. = *Journal of Hellenic Studies* (London).

l. = left. Used not in the heraldic sense, but from the spectator's point of view.

Mommsen-Blacas = Th. Mommsen: *Histoire de la Monnaie romaine* (trans. by Blacas and de Witte). Paris, 1865—1875.

Mon. Anc. = *Monumentum Ancyranum*, in the second edition of Mommsen (*Res gestae Divi Augusti*, Berlin, 1883).

Num. Chron. = *Numismatic Chronicle* (London).

Numism. Zeitschr. = *Numismatische Zeitschrift* (Vienna).

r. = right. Used not in the heraldic sense, but from the spectator's point of view.

Rev. Num. = *Revue Numismatique* (Paris).

Zeit. f. Num. = *Zeitschrift für Numismatik* (Berlin).

LIST OF PLATES

PLATE	I.	Nos. 1—3
,,	II.	Nos. 4, 5
,,	III.	No. 6, *obverse*
,,	IV.	No. 6, *reverse*
,,	V.	Nos. 7, 8 .
,,	VI.	Nos. 9—11
,,	VII.	No. 12, *obverse*
,,	VIII.	No. 12, *reverse*
,,	IX.	Nos. 13—27
,,	X.	Nos. 28—45
,,	XI.	Nos. 46—60
,,	XII.	Nos. 61—74
,,	XIII.	Nos. 75—88
,,	XIV.	Nos. 89—100
,,	XV.	Nos. 101—109

CONTENTS

	PAGE
PREFACE	v
GLOSSARY	ix
LIST OF ABBREVIATIONS	xiii
LIST OF PLATES	xvii

HISTORICAL ROMAN COINS:

1—3. The Earliest Roman Coinage: *circa* 338 B.C.	1
4—6. The Romanization of Campania: *circa* 312—290 B.C.	10
7—12. The Final Subjection of Italy: 290—269 B.C.	18
13—19. The Inauguration of an Imperial Coinage: 268 B.C.	27
20—24. The Crisis of the First Punic War: 242 B.C.	37
25. The Acquisition of Corcyra: 229 B.C.	44
26, 27. After Trasimene: 217 B.C.	46
28. Hannibal in Capua: 216—215 B.C.	50
29. M. Aemilius Lepidus and Ptolemaeus V.: 201 B.C.	51
30—32. Changes in the Denarius: 2nd cent. B.C.	56
33. C. Minucius Augurinus: *circa* 150—125 B.C.	62
34. T. Quinctius Flamininus: *circa* 124—103 B.C.	65
35—39. Charters of Liberty	66
40. The Surrender of Jugurtha by Bocchus: 106 or 105 B.C.	70
41, 42. Marius and the Barbarians: 104—101 B.C.	72
43, 44. C. Coelius Caldus, his achievements: 107—94 B.C.	75
45. The Corn Law of Saturninus: 100 B.C.	79
46, 47. The Social War: 90 B.C.	82
48—52. The Social War: 90—81 B.C.	85
53, 54. The Lex Papiria de asse semunciali: 89 B.C.	89
55. Sulla in Greece: 87—84 B.C.	92
56. Pompeius in Africa: 81 B.C.	94
57. The Subjection of King Aretas: 62 B.C.	98
58—60. Caesar in Rome: 49 B.C.	100
61, 62. The Senatorial Party in the Provinces: 49 B.C.	104
63. Caesar's Fourfold Triumph: 46 B.C.	107
64, 65. Corinth refounded: 44 B.C.	110

CONTENTS

	PAGE
66, 67. The Murder of Caesar: 44 B.C.	112
68—71. Brutus in Asia and Macedon: 43—42 B.C.	116
72—74. The Triumvirs: Nov. 43—Dec. 38 B.C.	118
75. Cassius at Rhodes: 43 B.C.	121
76, 77. The Legates of M. Antonius in Gaul: 42—41 B.C.	123
78, 79. Sextus Pompeius in Sicily: 42—36 B.C.	126
80. Q. Labienus Parthicus: 40 B.C.	128
81, 82. The Armenian Expedition of M. Antonius: 34 B.C.	131
83, 84. Octavian's Triumph: 29 B.C.	134
85, 86. Caesar Augustus: 27 B.C.	136
87—90. The Recovery of the Standards: 20 B.C.	138
91. The Province of Asia: 19 B.C.	143
92. Armenia Recepta: *circa* 19 B.C.	145
93, 94. The Secular Games: 17 B.C.	148
95, 96. The Public Roads: 17 B.C.	150
97—100. The Monetary Reform of Augustus: *circa* 15 B.C.	153
101—103. The Altar of Lyon: 10 B.C.	158
104. The Death of Nero Drusus: 9 B.C.	160
105, 106. The Senatorial Mint at Antioch: *circa* 7—6 B.C.	162
107. Gaius Caesar: *circa* 5 B.C.	165
108. Gaius and Lucius Caesares: *circa* 2 B.C.	168
109. The Pannonian Triumph of Tiberius: A.D. 13	171
INDEX	175

HISTORICAL ROMAN COINS

THE EARLIEST ROMAN COINAGE
CIRCA 338 B.C.

1. *Obv.* Bearded head of Janus; below, —; all on raised disk.

    Rev. Prow of galley r.; above, I; all on raised disk.

    Bronze *as* (cast). 294·97 grammes (4552·08 grains). B.M.C. I., p. 5, No. 1.

2. *Obv.* Beardless head of Hercules l., wearing lion-skin; behind, •••; all on raised disk.

    Rev. Prow of galley r.; below, •••; all on raised disk.

    Bronze *quadrans* (cast). 73·42 grammes (1133·04 grains). B.M.C. I., p. 9, No. 46.

3. *Obv.* Bearded head of Mars l., in crested helmet.

    Rev. Head of bridled horse r.; behind, ear of barley; below, on raised band, **ROMANO**.

    Silver *Campanian didrachm.* 7·45 grammes (115·0 grains). B.M.C. II., p. 121, No. 1.

Until comparatively recent times, it was usual to accept the tradition that coinage was introduced into Rome as early as the regal period, and this although some scholars, including Eckhel, the founder of numismatic study, had shown irrefutable reasons against so early a date. The tradition was that King Servius was the first to mark bronze with a type;[1] and that the type was some kind of cattle (*pecus*), whence was derived the name *pecunia*. Further, sums of money are mentioned in the Twelve Tables; and we find equivalents of fines in cattle fixed by the *lex Iulia Papiria* of 430 B.C. and other early laws, such as the *lex Tarpeia*, which equated the ox to 100 *asses*, the sheep to 10 *asses*.

Now these sums of money were not necessarily coins,[2] any more than were the shekels of the time of Abraham; they were merely weights of bronze. That is to say, they were not pieces of metal artificially shaped and officially marked with types in guarantee of quality and weight. Pliny's statement, again, that the type of the earliest Roman money represented cattle, is probably due to some misunderstanding of his authority, or to a false inference from the etymology of the word. If his authority for the statement was Timaeus, whom he quotes in the previous sentence, he may well have misunderstood the Greek. The only early Roman coin with a type in any way corresponding

[1] Plin. *N. H.* 33. 43: Servius rex primus signavit aes, antea rudi (i.e., amorphous bronze) usos Romae Timaeus tradit. signatum est nota pecudum, unde et pecunia appellata.

[2] See Samwer und Bahrfeldt, *Gesch. des älteren röm. Münzwesens* (1883), pp. 17 f.

to Pliny's description is one of the quadrilateral bricks which bears the figure of an ox—a rare piece, which cannot have had much currency. But there is a curious parallel to Pliny's statement in the belief of various Greek authorities (Plutarch, Pollux, and the scholiast on Aristophanes) that the type of the earliest Attic coins was an ox. It is quite possible that all these statements go back to a misunderstood original. Some writer perhaps was discussing the primitive method of estimating values in cattle, and the substitution for it, in later times, of a monetary medium. He was taken to mean that the earliest coins actually represented, pictorially as well as economically, certain quantities of cattle. So that Pliny may not himself have been initially responsible for what must be regarded as an error. "Même dans ses bévues," says M. Théodore Reinach,[1] "Pline n'est qu'un copiste."

The literary "authority" for the commencement of a Roman coinage earlier than the middle of the fourth century cannot possibly stand against the evidence of the coins themselves. Their style points unmistakably to the period indicated. The type of prow on the reverses is not archaic. Nor is there any subsequent sign of advance in style from an archaic to a mature art, such as would necessarily appear had the coinage begun before the art was fully developed, as it was about 400 B.C.

[1] *L'Histoire par les Monnaies*, p. 98.

HISTORICAL ROMAN COINS

Rome first took rank as the chief power in Italy about 350 B.C. The Latin League was reorganised, doubtless on terms much more favourable to Rome than had been the case before, in 358. In 354 she made a treaty with the Samnites. By 353 she had completed the subjugation of Southern Etruria. In 348, most important of all, came the treaty with the Carthaginians. The agreement with the Samnites broke down in 343, when Capua and other Campanian communities threw themselves into the arms of Rome. In two years the Samnites were forced to recognise Rome as the suzerain of the Campanian cities. About 340—338, the Campanians, especially the Capuans, received the *civitas sine suffragio*. The last rival to Roman supremacy on the Latin coast, the Volscian Antium, whose inhabitants were famous for their piratical propensities, fell at the close of the Latin War, and in 338 the beaks of the Antiate battleships became the ornament of the speakers' platform in the Roman forum.[1]

Partly because of the prestige which it confers, but still more because of the revenue which it produces, the right of coinage has almost always been one of the most jealously guarded prerogatives of political supremacy; and it was now imperatively necessary that Rome should come into line with the other Italian states which

---

[1] Plin. *N. H.* 34. 20: in suggestu rostra devictis Antiatibus fixerat (C. Maenius) anno urbis ccccxvi.

had coined money with their own types for more than a century, especially as some of these very states were by this time subject to her. The earliest Roman coinage[1] is accordingly dual, consisting partly of coins issued at Rome itself, partly of coins issued in Campania for currency in the Campanian dominion.

In Central Italy, excepting Etruria, there had hitherto been no coinage, although imported coins and local uncoined bronze doubtless circulated as a medium of exchange. Bronze, indeed, was, and long remained, the standard metal in these parts. It stood to silver in the relation of 1 to 120. At this rate, one silver Campanian didrachm of 7·58 grammes[2] would be equivalent in value to $3\frac{1}{3}$ pounds, or 3 didrachms to 10 pounds, of bronze of the Osco-Latin standard of 273 grammes to the pound.[3] This is an inconvenient and clumsy relation ; but it was the best that could be attained at the time, and was improved at the first opportunity.

[1] What follows is based on Haeberlin's brochure, *Systematik des ältesten römischen Münzwesens* (Berlin, 1905), which has revolutionised our ideas of the early Roman coinage, and produced comparative order out of chaos. His theory has been attacked by A. Sambon (*L'aes grave italico*, Milan, 1907) and M. C. Soutzo (*Les lourdes monnaies de bronze de l'Italie Centrale* in *Rev. Num.* 1907), but, as I think, without due appreciation of the weight of his arguments.

[2] This seems to have been the normal weight, although the majority of the extant specimens fall below it. See Haeberlin, *Die metrologischen Grundlagen der ält. mittelital. Münzsysteme* (*Zeit. f. Num.* xxvii.), pp. 60 f.

[3] $120 \times 7·58 = 909·60 = 3\frac{1}{3} \times 273·15$.

HISTORICAL ROMAN COINS

This pound or *libra* of 273 grammes,[1] containing 12 ounces or *unciae*, was the pound on which the system of the earliest Roman bronze was based, the coin corresponding to the *libra* being called the *as*. It will be noticed that the *as* No. 1 weighs a good deal more than the normal *libra*. Indeed, it used to be assumed that the basis of the earliest Roman coinage was the heavier ("new Roman") pound of 327·45 grammes,[1] but that for some reason the coins were almost always cast under weight.[2] But the average weight, as ascertained from more than 1100 specimens of the *as*, is 267·66 grammes, which, allowing for the loss of weight by the circulation to which extant specimens must have been subject, may well represent an effective weight of 273 grammes. The excessive weight of some specimens, such as No. 1, and the low weight of others, must be accounted for by the roughness of the primitive methods of regulating the capacity of the moulds in which the coins were cast.

The original Roman bronze coinage was of six denominations, all bearing the prow on the reverse, while on the obverse were the heads of different divinities; marks of value were placed on both sides. The system was as follows:

[1] On the origin of this pound and of the new Roman pound of 327·45 grammes, see Haeberlin, *op. cit.* pp. 44 f., and Lehmann-Haupt, *Zeit. f. Num.* xxvii., pp. 131 f.

[2] The heaviest specimens seldom exceed 11 ounces of this heavier pound.

HISTORICAL ROMAN COINS

As: obv. type, head of Janus; mark of value, I.

Semis: obv. type, head of Jupiter; mark of value, S.

Triens: obv. type, head of Minerva; mark of value, ••••.

Quadrans: obv. type, head of Hercules; mark of value, •••.

Sextans: obv. type, head of Mercurius; mark of value, ••.

Uncia: obv. type, head of Bellona; mark of value, •.

Janus, as the god of beginnings, leads the series, just as his month leads the year.[1] "Juno Moneta," it will be noticed, is conspicuous by her absence. How is this to be explained?

It must be remembered that during this period, in spite of the general advance, and whatever later Roman historians may say, the course of Rome's fortunes was not marked by unbroken prosperity. It is, indeed, probable that, when the Romans entered into their first treaty with Carthage, so far from the Carthaginians making overtures,[2] the Romans were themselves in need of assistance; in other words, of money. It is significant[3] that the goddess Moneta

---

[1] Macdonald, *Coin Types*, p. 182.

[2] Liv. vii. 27: Cum amicitiam ac societatem petentes venissent (Carthaginienses).

[3] On this subject, see Assmann's ingenious speculations in *Klio*, vi., pp. 477 ff.

is first mentioned in connexion with a battle against the Aurunci in the year 345, when L. Furius Camillus invoked her aid. The temple which he vowed to her was built and dedicated on the Capitol in 344.[1]

It is generally supposed that the connexion of the mint with the temple of Juno Moneta on the Capitol dates only from the third century.[2] But the evidence to this effect is inadequate. Whether we accept or reject the ingenious theory which explains the Latin word *moneta* as a corruption of the Punic *machanath* ("camp"), a legend inscribed on one of the most important currencies circulating in the Western Mediterranean in the fourth century,[3] is of no importance for our present purpose. There can be little doubt that *moneta* gave rather than owed its name to the goddess. *Moneta* is the personification of money; and if the idea she embodies was of Carthaginian origin, we can understand why she became identified with Juno.[4] We may take it, therefore, that the Roman mint was from the first

---

[1] Liv. vii. 28.

[2] Marquardt, *Römische Staatsverw.*, ii. p. 11. Suidas, *s.v.* Μονῆτα, says that the Romans, being short of money in the war against Pyrrhus, obtained it by following the counsel of Moneta, the "Adviser," in gratitude to whom they vowed to establish their mint in the temple of the goddess. This story is partly due to the false etymology from *monere*.

[3] Hill, *Coins of Ancient Sicily*, pp. 143 ff.

[4] Vergil, *Aen.* i. 671: Iunonia hospitia. The Carthaginian goddess is really Astarte.

attached to the temple on the Capitol. But in this still comparatively conservative period, it is not to be expected that the Romans should represent on their coinage a deity who was a somewhat unsubstantial personification.

The coins struck at the mint of Capua (possibly also at other Campanian mints, although these cannot have been important) consist of silver didrachms and *litrae* (each $\frac{1}{10}$th of a didrachm), and of bronze coins used as small change. This bronze money—like most bronze in the Greek as opposed to the Italian world— was mere token money; its weight does not correspond to its nominal value. The types of the Capuan coins are various. Besides those of No. 3 we have the head of Apollo, or of the young Hercules, a horse and star, or the wolf and twins, on the silver, and other types on the bronze coins. Some of them are difficult to explain. The horse's bust may have been suggested by a similar device on some of the Carthaginian coins mentioned above.[1] The horse and star together may represent the Dioscuri, who afterwards appear on the first silver coinage struck in Rome itself (Nos. 13—15). The inscription on these Capuan coins takes the Campanian or Oscan form **ROMANO**, corresponding to forms like **CALENO**,

---

[1] Hill, *Coins of Ancient Sicily*, Plate x., 6. This itself reminds us of the omen which decided the choice of the site of Carthage (Vergil, *Aen.* i. 442).

HISTORICAL ROMAN COINS

SVESANO, found on autonomous coins of the cities of Campania.[1]

The first stage of the Roman coinage lasted down to 314 or 312, when the Samnite attempts to wrest Campania from the Romans were finally defeated, a dangerous revolt in Capua itself was crushed, and the Via Appia, connecting Rome with Capua, completed.

THE ROMANIZATION OF CAMPANIA.
Circa 312—290 B.C.

4. *Obv.* Head of Roma r., wearing Phrygian helmet; behind, II; all on raised disk.

Rev. Archaic wheel of six spokes; between two of them, II; all on raised disk.

Cast bronze *dupondius*. 600·24 grammes (9263 grains). B.M.C. Italy, p. 53, No. 1.

5. *Obv.* Head of Roma r., wearing Phrygian helmet; behind, a cornucopiæ.

Rev. Victory fastening a taenia to a palm branch; behind, **ROMANO**; in front, **T**.

Silver *didrachm*. 6·62 grammes (102·2 grains). B.M.C. II., p. 126, No. 36.

6. *Obv.* Eagle to front, displayed, holding thunderbolt in its talons.

---

[1] R. S. Conway, however (*Italic Dialects*, i. p. 144), thinks this form, in the inscriptions where Latin letters are employed, may be Latin.

HISTORICAL ROMAN COINS

Rev. Pegasus galloping l; below, [R]OMANOM

Cast bronze "brick,' 1389·63 grammes (21445 grains). B.M.C. I., p. 3, No. 2.

The second stage in the development of the Roman coinage is marked by a great extension of the functions of the Capuan mint.[1] At Rome itself little change seems to have taken place. Only the mark of value disappears from the obverse of the *as;* towards the end of the period the lowest denomination (*uncia*) is discontinued, and the prow is turned to the left instead of to the right. These changes are insignificant. But in Campania, in addition to four issues of silver didrachms (such as No. 5), not to mention drachms and small bronze, which continue with modifications the issues of the previous period, we now find certain series of heavy bronze or *aes grave* (such as No. 4), certain single issues of bar-money or quadrilateral "bricks" (such as No. 6), and also perhaps even gold coins. But the gold issues more probably began for the first time in the next period (No. 11).

The silver didrachm of this series[2] weighs 6·82 grammes normal, and is the equivalent of

[1] The dating and historical interpretation of the coins described in this section, as in the preceding and in the following, are in all essentials due to Haeberlin's *Systematik*.

[2] The T on the reverse is a series mark, employed by the mint officials to distinguish the various dies, or batches of coins. In this series, beginning with A, the marks run right through the Greek alphabet and then begin again with AA and once more exhaust the alphabet to ΩΩ.

6 silver scruples or *scripula* of Roman weight. At the rate of 120 to 1 the didrachm would correspond in value to 3 *asses* of bronze,[1] and it is significant that the highest known denomination of the series of coins to which No. 4 belongs is not an *as*, but a *tressis* or piece of 3 *asses*. The connexion of this wheel-series (as, from the constant reverse type, it is called) of *aes grave* with the silver series is further established by the community of obverse types, and by other smaller points of contact. The connexion of the quadrilateral bricks with the silver is less certain, but may be regarded as probable. On the brick No. 6 is the inscription **ROMANOM**. It can therefore hardly be later than this first issue of silver (No. 5) in this period, for the subsequent issues have not **ROMANO** or **ROMANOM**, but **ROMA**. On all the other varieties of bricks the inscription is wanting. This brick (No. 6) might, it has been urged, equally well belong to the first period of the Roman coinage.[2] Such an arrangement, however, would leave the first issue of silver in the present period without any corresponding brick; whereas, on the system described above, each of the four issues of silver in this period would have its corresponding brick.

The helmet worn by Roma—for that Roma is

---

[1] $6 \cdot 82 \times 120 = 818 \cdot 40 = 3 \times 272 \cdot 80$.
[2] Regling, in *Klio*, vi. p. 500.

HISTORICAL ROMAN COINS

intended admits of no doubt[1]—is of the "Phrygian" type; it is crested, and its point ends in a small griffin's head. This form of helmet seems to convey an allusion to the legendary foundation of Rome by exiles from Troy. It has already been suggested that the reverse type of the earliest Romano-Campanian didrachm (the horse's head) may have been inspired by a Carthaginian model. And here again our Roman type reminds us, though somewhat faintly, of the fine head of a queen wearing a tiara (not a helmet) of Asiatic form, on certain other Carthaginian pieces.[2] The Victory, as symbolical of the continued advance of the Roman power, is obviously appropriate to the occasion of issue.

The reverse type of the new *aes grave* of the Capuan mint—a wheel—has been ingeniously explained as a symbol of the internal communication which was established between Rome and Capua by the completion of the Appian Way. It thus forms a sort of parallel to the prow on the Roman *aes grave*, which symbolized the newly acquired command of the sea.[3]

The quadrilateral brick is one of a class of pieces which numismatists have as a rule conspired to call *aes signatum*, keeping the term *aes grave* for the circular coins, while the most primitive amorphous

[1] See Haeberlin in *Corolla Numismatica* (1906), pp. 135 ff., p. 146, etc.
[2] Hill, *Coins of Ancient Sicily*, pl. x. 7.
[3] Haeberlin, *Systematik*, p. 32, where an analogy from an imperial coin is quoted.

metal currency is called *aes rude*. To the last term no exception whatever can be taken. But, strictly speaking, any *aes* marked with a type—whatever its form—is *signatum*. Since, as we now know, the quadrilateral pieces did not belong to the earliest period of Roman coinage, the restriction to them of the term *aes signatum* is even less justifiable than it was when they were supposed to represent the transition from the amorphous to the circular coins.

On the piece at present before us the eagle, as the attribute of Jupiter and the symbol of Roman sovereignty,[1] has a general appropriateness. Of the Pegasus, on the other hand, no certain explanation has been offered. The Romans must recently have become familiar with it as a coin-type, for " Pegasi " on the Corinthian model[2] had been struck in large quantities since the middle of the fourth century at the South Italian city of Locri and at Syracuse, and in less numbers at small mints, such as Mesma and Rhegium in Bruttium and Leontini in Sicily. Roman relations with the eastern shores of the Adriatic were not as yet very close, but the " Pegasi " of the various mints in that part of the world, and of Corinth itself, must have been common in Italy. This, then, may have suggested the type. If so, it is improbable that it has any special mythological significance here.

[1] This idea, however, may be of later origin.
[2] See *Hist. Gr. Coins*, pp. 85 f.

HISTORICAL ROMAN COINS

These "bricks," regarded as money, are only surpassed in awkwardness[1] by the enormous bronze coins of necessity issued in Sweden in comparatively modern times. But were they really coins after all? The weights of the extant specimens vary from 1830 to 1142 grammes. They never, like the contemporary circular money, bear marks of value. They very frequently occur in fragments, having been, it seems, deliberately broken. It is doubtful, therefore, whether they were actual money. It has been suggested[2] that they were issued by the mint to serve all purposes hitherto served by the *aes rude* and the typeless bars of metal, except the one purpose of monetary exchange. Bronze was used, for instance, to dedicate to the gods, or to place with the dead to furnish them with means for their journey into the other world, or to supply their needs when arrived there; it played a part in various legal acts, such as *emtio-venditio per aes et libram*. An alternative suggestion[3] is that they were issued as a sort of raw material, which could be used in large payments together with ordinary circular bronze. The types impressed upon them would serve to guarantee the quality of the metal of which they

---

[1] We are reminded of the passage in Livy (iv. 60) in which the Romans are described as *aes grave plaustris ad aerarium convehentes*, because *argentum signatum* did not yet exist. This was when the military pay was introduced in the Volscian War at the end of the fifth century, *i.e.*, before the Romans had any coined money at all!

[2] Haeberlin, *op. cit.*, pp. 56 f.

[3] Regling in *Klio, ut sup.*, p. 501.

HISTORICAL ROMAN COINS

were made. Of course the scales would still be necessary. There is ample evidence that in the Middle Ages bars of metal, stamped and issued officially by various mints, were used together with ordinary coins; and it is not improbable that the Roman gold bars of the end of the third and the fourth century of our era often played a similar part. Nevertheless, it must not be forgotten that these bars, both in late Roman and in mediæval times, were made of the more precious metals then in circulation. Whereas, when the bronze bricks were used, we know that an official silver coinage existed. Thus, since, in the period which we are now considering, the silver didrachm was worth three *asses*, a couple of such didrachms would have more than served the purpose, from the point of view of exchange value, of one of these unwieldy bricks. It is possible to urge that in some of the central districts the silver Romano-Campanian coinage would perhaps be scarce; that, if the *aes grave* issued at the Capuan mint was intended specially for the Latin district, the Capuan silver would be more or less restricted to Campania. We may also be reminded of the fact that, in the sacred well at Vicarello, heaps of the struck Romano-Campanian bronze occurred together with all sorts of bronze coins,[1] but no Romano-Campanian silver.

For the significance of the fact that the Romano-Campanian money circulated farther north, see Haeberlin in *Zeit. f. Num.* xxvi. p. 235.

HISTORICAL ROMAN COINS

This, however, proves little, for silver is seldom found in sacred deposits.[1] It must, at the same time, be admitted that Romano-Campanian silver rarely occurs in hoards from Central Italy, although the struck bronze of the same class does so frequently.[2] The question of the use of the "bricks" must, therefore, for the present, be left open; we cannot disprove the theory that they may have been used in large payments, but the theory that they served ceremonial purposes is by far the most plausible that has yet been advanced. It is just in such usages that we should look for the survival of a somewhat clumsy and inconvenient form.

In the coinage of this period, even as thus briefly outlined, we see a striking reflection of the gradual Romanization of Campania and Latium. The silver is issued on a Roman standard, based on the scruple of 1·137 grammes, which is the equivalent of half a pound of bronze. The relation between the bronze and silver coinage becomes convenient and harmonious, the incongruity of the preceding period being abolished. The apparently Campanian genitive **ROMANO** is superseded, after the first issue, by

---

[1] Mommsen-Blacas, *Hist. de la Monn. rom.* I., p. 174.

[2] The statements of Marchi and Tessieri (*L'aes grave del Mus. Kircheriano*, p. 66) are somewhat vague in regard to the metal of the coins from "New Latium," and in the other hoards mentioned by A. Sambon (*L'aes grave Italico*, pp. 11, 12) the Romano-Campanian issues represented are all of bronze.

HISTORICAL ROMAN COINS

ROMA. The personification of Roma herself appears as the leading type. At least one of the other types conveys a direct allusion to the binding together of Rome and Capua by the Appian Way.

It is perhaps more than a coincidence that, as Haeberlin reminds us, the year of the censorship of the greatest Roman of the age, Appius Claudius Caecus, is the year to which, on independent grounds, the reform of the Capuan mint can best be assigned. It is clear that a far-reaching reform like this could not have been instituted without his consent; and it is reasonable to suppose that the man who joined Capua to Rome by road also helped to consolidate the young Roman empire by the highly important economic measure which we have just discussed.

THE FINAL SUBJECTION OF ITALY.
290—269 B.C.

7. *Obv.* Head of Bellona l., wearing crested Athenian helmet; behind, •

   Rev. Prow r.; above, **ROMA**; below, •

   Bronze *uncia*, 13·48 grammes (208 grains). B.M.C. I., p. 22, No. 91.

8. *Obv.* Head of beardless Janus on raised disk; above, I.

   Rev. Head of Mercurius l. in winged petasus, on raised disk; above, I.

   Cast bronze *as*. 339·25 grammes (5235·4 grains). British Museum (Parkes Weber gift).

HISTORICAL ROMAN COINS

9. *Obv.* Head of Apollo r., hair bound with diadem, on raised disk; [above, **I**].

Rev. Similar type l.; above, **I**.

Cast bronze *as*. 346·02 grammes (5340 grains). B.M.C. *Italy*, p. 51, No. 1.

10. *Obv.* Head of Janus, beardless, laureate.

Rev. Jupiter, with thunderbolt and sceptre, in four-horse chariot r., driven by Victory; below, in sunk letters on a raised tablet, **ROMA**.

Silver *quadrigatus didrachm*. 6·52 grammes (100·6 grains). B.M.C. II., p. 133, No. 90.

11. *Obv.* Similar type to No. 10; below, **XXX**.

Rev. Two soldiers taking an oath over the body of a pig, held by a kneeling attendant; below, **ROMA**.

Gold piece of 30 *asses*. 4·47 grammes (69 grains). British Museum.

12. *Obv.* Elephant r.

Rev. Sow l.

Cast bronze "brick." 1746·49 grammes (26952 grains). B.M.C *Italy*, p. 62, No. 1.

The Samnites, whose power was broken at the battle of Sentinum in 295 B.C., continued the struggle against Rome until they were forced to conclude peace in 290. The third phase of the early Roman coinage is probably to be dated approximately from this time. The introduction of the *denarius* in 269 or 268 gives us the lower limit.

The first historical fact which we must bear in

mind is the establishment by Rome of an effectual control over the whole of Central Italy. By 283 the Sabine country had been annexed, colonies like Hatria established on the Adriatic coast, and the Kelts, who threatened from the North, decisively defeated. Secondly, this settlement was followed by a displacement of the forces towards the South. The barbarians of Central Italy began to press hardly on the Greek cities of Magna Graecia. The Romans, urged to interfere, effectively restored order, established garrisons in Locri and other cities, and drove the Tarentines, jealous of their position, into war. The success of Rome in the struggle with Tarentum and Pyrrhus left her mistress of practically the whole of Italy.

This is a period, then, of transition. Out of a state, powerful indeed, but still not so powerful that other Italian states can only despair of success in a struggle with her, Rome is developing into the undisputed ruler of the peninsula. The coinage likewise passes through a transitory phase: various experiments seem to be made; the system is complicated, half-hearted, and lacks uniformity; and it is only after more than twenty years of this unsatisfactory state of things that Rome takes the heroic step of sweeping aside her rivals in the coinage. She issues her own silver, which henceforth—with but few exceptions—is the only silver currency of Italy.

HISTORICAL ROMAN COINS

The first innovation in the coinage of the Roman mint which attracts our notice in this period is a reduction in the weight of the *as*. Opinions vary much as to the degree of this reduction. The actual weights of the *asses* of this "older reduction" vary from 156·65 to 99·60 grammes, with an average of 131·23 grammes. The *semisses* vary from 89·50 to 57·96 grammes, with an average of 73·16 grammes.[1] If we are to suppose that there was throughout this period a normal weight for the *as*, and that the old Osco-Latin pound was still in use, we are almost bound to accept the view that the weight was 136·5 grammes, *i.e.*, half the old *libra*. The new *as* would then be the equivalent of the scruple of silver. But, when we consider the smaller denominations of this period, from the *triens* down to the quarter-*uncia*, a curious fact emerges. The normal weights indicate that, if we assume an *as* of 136·5 grammes normal, it was divided not duodecimally, as before, but decimally. Thus the normal *uncia* weighs apparently not 11·37 but 13·64 grammes (actual average 12·85 grammes), *i.e.*, $\frac{1}{10}$ of the *as* of 136·5 grammes. How are we to explain the sudden supersession of the duodecimal by the decimal system?

It is due to the fact[2] that the bronze coinage was

---

[1] Regling, *ut sup.*, p. 495.
[2] See Haeberlin, *Metrol. Grundlagen*, pp. 104 f.; also his *Systematik*, p. 39.

now regarded as subordinate to the silver; the semi-libral *as* was merely the equivalent in bronze of the silver scruple. Now in the Romano-Campanian silver system the unit, or scruple, was divided decimally into ten *libellae*; the actual denominations were all issued in bronze, in the shape of pieces of 4, 3, 2 *libellae*, 1 *libella* and ½ *libella*. Since the dominant unit, the silver scruple, was divided decimally, it is not surprising that the subordinate unit, the bronze *as*, was divided in the same way.

Such being the relation between the two units, the reduction of the *as* was a matter of course; it and the other denominations were bound in time to become a sort of token-money, although we do not know that any restriction was placed on the amount of such coin which could be tendered at a time. The reduction of the bronze has been regarded as a sign of state-bankruptcy; but it was nothing of the kind, so long as the bronze was covered by the silver issues of the state. This being so, why should the government have been at pains to fix the weight of the bronze coins? The reason was that the ordinary Roman, if he was like the ordinary modern, would never really understand the nature of token-money. A reduction in the size of the British penny would be quite enough to produce a popular outcry and shake the public confidence. In order to reassure the public, therefore, it may well be that the Roman state pretended, from time to time,

HISTORICAL ROMAN COINS

to regulate the weight of the *as*, while allowing it gradually to sink. But the evidence of the coins themselves shows that any such action can have been little more than a pretence.

We must not leave the question of the first reduction of the *as* without mentioning Haeberlin's suggestion that it was associated with a public remission of debts. By the reduction of the weight of the *as*, debtors would be proportionately relieved. Now, about the beginning of our present period (288—286) the Plebs, after long and serious disturbances on account of debt, seceded to the Janiculum; they returned at the instance of the dictator Q. Hortensius.[1] It is quite possible that they returned only on condition of the remission of their debts by some such measure as the halving of the *as*. If so, the beginning of our period must be fixed in 286 B.C.[2]

The reduction in the weight, and therefore in the size, of the bronze coins brought about a technical change. The *uncia* No. 7, unlike the pieces of *aes grave* with which we have met so far, is struck, not cast. It is a difficult matter to make dies of a large size strong enough to stand the strain of striking. Thanks to the reduction, it became possible for the Romans to produce by striking not only the *uncia*, $\frac{1}{2}$ *uncia*, and $\frac{1}{4}$ *uncia*, but also the *sextans* or piece of

---

[1] Liv. *Epit. libri* xi.
[2] Haeberlin, *Systematik*, pp. 44 f.

HISTORICAL ROMAN COINS

2 *unciae*. The higher denominations continued to be made with moulds, until the further reduction brought these also within the range of the engraver of dies.

Two series of *aes grave*, other than the ordinary Roman series just considered, were produced in this period. They are known as the heavy Janus-Mercurius and the heavy Apollo series,[1] from the types of the *asses* in each (see Nos. 8, 9). Coins of the former series are characterized by bad workmanship and rudeness of style, by comparatively low relief, by a weight based on the pound of 327·45 grammes,[2] and by a greyish granular oxide common in the district round Rome; they also occur in the famous deposit of Vicarello in much greater quantities than the Apollo series (1109 as against 108 pieces). The coins of the Apollo series, on the other hand, are of good style—unusually good for *aes grave*—and in high relief, conform to a different standard (a pound of 341 grammes),[3] and have the fine smooth green or brown patina characteristic of Campania. The Apollo series is accordingly assigned to the Capuan mint, the Janus-Mercurius series to the Roman. The head of

---

[1] To be distinguished from the light series with corresponding types, and symbols (sickle and vine-leaf) on their reverses; these belong to the previous period.

[2] Both Nos. 8 and 9 are above the normal weights, as is often the case with *aes grave*. Cp. Haeberlin, *Metrolog. Grundlagen*, p. 41.

[3] See Haeberlin, *Metrolog. Grundlagen*, p. 21.

HISTORICAL ROMAN COINS

Janus on these coins is beardless, not bearded as on the prow series. We find the same head on the earliest Capuan silver and gold, with which we shall deal presently.[1]

Thus we now see the pound of 327·45 grammes (with the scruple of 1·137 grammes as its $\frac{1}{288}$ part) definitely established in Rome.

At Capua, the only silver coins issued in this period are the well-known *quadrigati* (No. 10), struck on the same standard as their predecessors. The types, it is to be observed, are purely Roman. The Capuan mint also issued large quantities of struck bronze of smaller denominations, the *libella*, its multiples (up to 4) and its half.

More remarkable are the gold coins (No. 11)—the first issued under Roman authority—which accompanied the silver *quadrigati*. They have a similar obverse, but on the reverse is a representation of two soldiers taking an oath over the body of a sacrificed swine. There are three denominations, the didrachm weighing 6 scruples, a piece weighing 4 scruples, and the drachm of 3 scruples. On the piece of 4 scruples (No. 11) appears a mark of value, **XXX**, showing it to be equal to 30 *asses*. These are supposed to be 30 *asses* of Italic weight, *i.e.*, of 273 grammes each. This may well be so,

---

[1] The lack of a beard on this double head is not sufficient reason for assuming it to represent some deity other than Janus.

for, although the new pound may have now come in at Rome, there would be nothing surprising in the retention of the older pound, as a unit of reckoning at least, in Campania.[1]

Of the various "bricks" which are attributed to this period, one (No. 12), is of peculiar interest, for it is impossible to deny that in some way or other it must be associated with the war with Pyrrhus. Legend says that at the battle of Ausculum in 279 B.C. the elephants of Pyrrhus were frightened by the grunting of swine on the Roman side.[2] The five elephants taken later at the battle of Beneventum were led in triumph in 273, and it was probably on this occasion, when elephants were first seen in Rome, that the piece was issued at Capua.[3] Whether the story of the swine is true, or had already been invented by that time, or was even a later growth, inspired by the types of the "brick," who shall say?

---

[1] The extremely difficult problems connected with this early gold coinage have been discussed by Haeberlin (*Zeit. f. Num.* xxvi., pp. 229 f.). In particular he has rehabilitated the piece of 30 *asses*, which was generally supposed to be false.—The equation of 4 scruples of gold to 30 *asses* of bronze of the Italic weight gives a ratio of 1820 : 1 as between gold and bronze, and if silver was to bronze as 120 : 1, of $15\frac{1}{6}$: 1 as between gold and silver. $30 \times 273 = 8190 =$ approximately $1820 \times 1\cdot137 \times 4$; and $1820 = 120 \times 15\frac{1}{6}$.

[2] Aelian *de nat. anim.* I. 38.

[3] Haeberlin, *Systematik*, p. 54.

HISTORICAL ROMAN COINS

THE INAUGURATION OF AN IMPERIAL COINAGE.
268 B.C.

13. *Obv.* Head of Roma r. in winged helmet, ornamented with griffin's head; behind, **X**.
Rev. The Dioscuri on horseback, charging r.; below, on tablet, **ROMA**.

Silver *denarius*. 4·32 grammes (66·7 grains). B.M.C. I., p. 15, No. 6.

14. Similar to preceding, but **V** instead of **X** on obv., and **ROMA** on rev.

Silver *quinarius*. 2·03 grammes (31·3 grains). B.M.C. I., p. 15, No. 10.

15. Similar to No. 13, but **I·IS** instead of **X**, and **ROMA**.

Silver *sestertius*. 1·07 grammes (16·5 grains). B.M.C. I., p. 16, No. 13.

16. *Obv.* Head of Janus, laureate; above, **I**.
Rev. Prow r.; above **I**; below, **ROMA**.

Struck bronze *as*. 43·16 grammes (666 grains). B.M.C. I., p. 29, No. 219.

17. *Obv.* Bust of Jupiter r. laureate; behind, **S**.
Rev. Prow r.; below, **ROMA**; above, **S**.

Struck bronze *semis*. 20·41 grammes (315 grains). B.M.C. I., p. 31, No. 232.

18. *Obv.* Head of Roma r., in winged helmet; behind, **V**.

HISTORICAL ROMAN COINS

Rev. The Dioscuri charging r.; below their horses, ⱴ; in exergue, **ROMA**.

Silver *quinarius*. 2·11 grammes (32·6 grains). B.M.C. II., p. 179, No. 151.

19. *Obv.* Head of Jupiter r. laureate.

Rev. Victory crowning a trophy; in exergue, **ROMA**.

Silver *victoriatus*. 3·22 grammes (49·7 grains). B.M.C. I., p. 36, No. 296.

"Imperial" is not too grand an epithet for the coinage on the new system inaugurated by Rome in 269–8 B.C. The *denarius*, at first intended as the standard coin of the Italian possessions, spread with the extension of the Roman dominions beyond the seas, and eventually dominated the currency of the civilized world for more than five hundred years. Not until the end of the third century after Christ, when it had sunk, it is true, to be a pitiable reflection of the excellent money as which it began, was it finally superseded by a new silver denomination. All through the Middle Ages the name persisted, and its initial still provides the abbreviation for the English "penny."

We are fortunate in knowing within a couple of years the date of the great reform. Pliny's reckoning —which is circumstantially stated—gives us 269 B.C.[1]

---

[1] *N. H.* 33. 13 (44): Argentum signatum anno urbis cccclxxxv, Q. Ogulnio C. Fabio cos., quinque annis ante primum Punicum bellum.

HISTORICAL ROMAN COINS

The Epitome of Livy[1] places the change between the foundation of the colonies of Ariminum and Beneventum on the one hand, and the subjection of the Umbrians and Sallentines on the other. The two colonies in question were founded in 268 B.C.; the wars with the Umbrians and Sallentines seem to have gone on during 267 and 266. It may be that the rogation introducing the reform dated from 269, the coinage itself from the next year. It would take some time, when once the law was passed, to organize the Roman mint for the production of silver. Engravers would have to be fetched from Capua, and new workshops for striking coins installed. Hitherto few but cast coins had been issued from Rome. If the law was passed late in 269, it would be surprising if the coins were issued before 268.[2]

The *denarius* was, as its name implies, the silver equivalent of 10 bronze *asses;* hence its mark of value, **X**. Similarly the *quinarius* (marked **V**), and the *sestertius* or *semis-tertius* (marked **IIS**), are the equivalents of 5 and 2½ *asses* respectively.[3] Let us for the moment

---

et placuit denarium pro decem libris aeris valere, quinarium pro quinque, sestertium pro dupondio ac semisse.

[1] *Epit. lib.* xv.: Coloniae deductae Ariminum in Piceno, Beneventum in Samnio. tunc primum populus Romanus argento uti coepit. Umbri et Sallentini victi, etc.

[2] A certain amount of confirmation of the date 268 is to be gathered from an independent passage of Pliny relating to the coinage of 217 B.C., which we shall discuss later.

[3] The dividing dot between the two units in the *sestertius* mark has

assume that when the *denarius* was introduced the weight of the *as* was fixed by law. The normal weight of the earliest *denarius* is 4·55 grammes (4 scruples). At the rate of 120 : 1, it would be equivalent to 546 grammes of bronze, or 10 pieces of 54·6 grammes. The *as* of the time must therefore have weighed 54·6 grammes, which is $\frac{1}{6}$ (the *sextans*) of the pound of 327·45 grammes. In other words, the *as* of the original *denarius* system was of the sextantal standard.

There is, however, a certain body of opinion in favour of the view that the *as* had not fallen quite so low at the time of the introduction of the *denarius*, and that it belonged not to the sextantal but to the triental standard; that is to say, that the *denarius* was the equivalent in value of 10 *asses* of 109·15 grammes. Such an equation postulates a ratio between silver and bronze of no less than 240 : 1.[1] We should therefore have to assume that, when the *denarius* was instituted, silver was forced up in value to twice as much as it had been hardly a generation before. There is nothing incredible in this, since, as we have seen, silver was now the dominant partner in the system, and the bronze coin was little more than a token. Still, so violent a change in the ratio between

---

been combined with them so as to give the sign HS generally used in texts for *sestertius*.

[1] $1091·5 = 239·8 \times 4·55$.

the metals would probably have excited apprehension, and it is much more probable that when the *denarius* was introduced the bronze *as* had actually fallen to so low a weight that the equation was possible with the old ratio of 120 : 1.

The triental system, it has been argued, must have been in force in 268, since as late as 246, when the Roman colony of Brundusium was founded, the coinage of that place was instituted on the triental standard. Mommsen maintained that, if this Roman colony issued coins on the triental standard at the time of its foundation, that standard must have then been in use at Rome itself. But it is impossible to insist on such an argument, in view of our scanty knowledge of the relative values of bronze and silver in Calabria at this time. On that relation partly, and not wholly on the relation in force at Rome, would depend the standard adopted for the bronze coinage in the new colony. Or, it may well be that, in order to spread the influence of the *denarius*, the Romans gave it a forced value in their colonies, such as they could not afford to give to it at Rome itself. If a *denarius* was worth 10 triental *asses* in Brundusium, and only 10 sextantal *asses* in Rome, *denarii* would tend to flow towards the colony.

A very doubtful support is given to Mommsen's theory by the statement of Pliny[1] that the weight of

[1] *N. H.* 33. 44.

the *as* was reduced during the first Punic War. Pliny indeed leads one to suppose that the libral weight had been maintained up to then, and that it was suddenly lowered to the sextantal. In view of the weights of the extant coins, this is either nonsense, or to be interpreted as meaning that the reduced weight was not legally recognized until the sextantal stage was reached. Pliny's statement is so far in favour of Mommsen's theory that it implies that the sextantal stage was first legally recognized during the first Punic War. But we have seen what a serious difficulty is caused by supposing that the legal *as* was more than sextantal when the *denarius* was introduced. It is quite likely that Pliny may have been anxious to find an honourable excuse for the reduction of the *as*—unnecessarily, since, as we have seen, the reduction was a natural development and not a symptom of state bankruptcy—and so hit upon the stress of the first Punic War as offering circumstances sufficiently straitened. The probabilities, however, are all in favour of the sextantal *as* having been legalized when the *denarius* was introduced. Up till that time, since the mint at Rome issued no silver, it may not have seemed so necessary to fix the weight of the *as*, although the number of *asses* which went to the silver unit was doubtless constant. But when both silver and bronze began to be issued from Rome it would obviously be desirable not merely to define

HISTORICAL ROMAN COINS

the exchange, but also to determine by law the weight of the bronze money.

We have seen that in the previous period the *as* was divided decimally. With the introduction of the *denarius* system a return was made to the duodecimal division. "From the moment when in the capital the clear principle of a parallel double standard took the place of a fluctuation between a silver standard and the expression thereof in bronze, the *denarius* was divided into ten *asses*, the *as* into twelve *unciae*."[1] That is to say, each metal was now coined on its natural divisional system.

The head of Roma[2] on the new silver coinage is considerably altered from the form in which the early Capuan silver showed it. The helmet is no longer "Phrygian"; it is of the ordinary round shape with visor, provided, however, with wings and with a griffin-headed crest such as decorated the old "Phrygian" helmet. This, with slight modifications, long continues to be the usual head-dress of Roma, although the Phrygian form is occasionally revived.

The Dioscuri are represented charging, as the later Roman tradition conceived their *epiphania* at the battle of Lake Regillus in 496 B.C. The older tradition, preserved by Livy, seems to have been merely that

---

[1] Haeberlin, *Metrol. Grundlagen*, p. 105.
[2] Certainly not Minerva. See Haeberlin, *Der Roma-Typus*, in *Corolla Numismatica*, pp. 135—155.

HISTORICAL ROMAN COINS

Aulus Postumius vowed a temple to Castor. But before the *denarius* was introduced Pollux had become the inseparable twin-brother of Castor, in accordance with the Greek conception of the pair, and perhaps also with the legend of their intervention at the battle of the Sagra on the side of the Locrians against the Crotoniates.[1] But apart from all this the significance of the type, from a monetary point of view, lies in the fact that the Dioscuri were the tutelary divinities of the Roman knights, *i.e.*, of that class of the sovereign people who were especially occupied with commerce, so that their temple was in the heart of the business quarter.[2]

The reduction of the *as* to one-sixth of the original weight, and the corresponding reduction of the smaller denominations, brought them all down to a diameter (the *as* measuring about an inch and a half) which made it possible to strike them with dies instead of casting them in moulds. In the previous period this had not been possible for denominations larger than the *triens*. Some of the latest of the cast coins, by their grotesque rudeness, offer a curious contrast to the struck pieces.

What was the effect on the coinage of Italy in general of the important changes which we have

---

[1] Justin xx. 3. Bethe in Pauly-Wissowa, *Realencyclop.* V. 1105. The battle took place about 520 B.C.

[2] Mommsen-Blacas, ii., p. 29; Macdonald, *Coin Types*, p. 183.

described? Capua continued to issue the silver *quadrigati*, perhaps even as late as the Hannibalian War; but the issue was limited, and the metal eventually adulterated. Elsewhere in Italy the local silver coinage came to an end, with one or two exceptions. Of these the most important was the coinage of the Bruttians, which was continued down to the Hannibalian War. It is possible that Tarentum and Neapolis also continued their silver currency in a limited measure.[1] In regard to bronze, the local mints, so far as we know, were little, if at all, restricted. To compensate for the cessation of the independent coinage of silver, the Romans established mints for coinage on the *denarius* system in various places, such as Hatria, Croton, Luceria. Some of these issues can be identified by mint-marks: thus the *quinarius* No. 18 is attributed to Luceria on the ground of the letter ↳ (for L), which it bears. In other cases the local coinage is distinguished merely by its somewhat ruder workmanship, and cannot be assigned to specific mints.

But in addition to the local issues of coins on the *denarius* system, the Romans established, either about the same time or a little later,[2] a currency which is represented by the *victoriatus* (No. 19). The reason

[1] See A. J. Evans, *The "Horsemen" of Tarentum*, pp. 165 f.

[2] The date generally accepted is 229 B.C., when Corcyra, Apollonia, and Dyrrhachium submitted to Rome, retaining however some considerable measure of autonomy. Mommsen-Blacas, ii., p. 93.

for the name is clear from the type of the reverse. The normal weight of the *victoriatus* in the first period of its existence was ¾ of the *denarius*, *i.e.*, 3 scruples or 3·41 grammes. It was, however, regarded not as a denomination subordinate to the *denarius*, but as a unit by itself; witness the fact that its half was marked with S, just as was the half *as*. What is more, from the purely Roman point of view, it was not looked upon as a regular coin. It is the only piece not marked with its value. It follows that, though it had of course a commercial value, it was not legal tender. "A man who was owed 300 *denarii* could be forced to take 600 *quinarii* or 1200 *sesterces*, but not 400 *victoriati*."[1] It was, as Pliny says, treated *mercis loco*.[2] Why was this?

The fact is that the *victoriatus* took the place of the Campanian drachm, the half of the *quadrigatus* didrachm, the drachm having ceased to be issued before its double, which, as we have said, lingered on until nearly the end of the century. The *victoriatus* weighed the same as the drachm which it succeeded, and was struck in all the local Roman mints—Luceria, Vibo Valentia, Croton, Corcyra and the like. It also weighed the same as certain currencies of important trading cities in Illyricum, viz., Apollonia and Dyrrhachium. Whether the *victoriatus* or the Illyric

---

[1] Mommsen-Blacas, ii., p. 87.
[2] *N. H.* 33. 46.

coinages on this standard came first we cannot know. In either case, the uniformity of system points to the importance of trade between Italy and the Illyric coast. But the way in which Roman influence was, through the Romano-Campanian coinage, pervading the Mediterranean coast is also shown by the facts that the latest Tarentine didrachms are based on a standard of 6 scruples, and that a great trading port like Massalia found it desirable to assimilate its standard to that of the Romano-Campanian 3-scruple drachm.

The *victoriatus*, then, was not part of the home coinage properly speaking, but a kind of feeler thrown out by Rome before she decided to make the *denarius* itself a world coinage. When she found herself able to do this, she abolished the *victoriatus* as a separate denomination, by equating it to the *quinarius*. This was effected by the Clodian law, about 104 B.C.[1]

THE CRISIS OF THE FIRST PUNIC WAR.

242 B.C.

20. *Obv.* Bust of Mars, r. wearing crested helmet, behind, ↓X.

Rev. Eagle r. on thunderbolt, flapping its wings; below, ROMA.

Gold. 60 sesterce piece. 3·41 grammes (52·6 grains). B.M.C. I., p. 27, No. 185.

[1] On the significance of the *victoriatus*, as outlined above, see Haeberlin in *Zeit. f. Num.* xxvi., p. 238.

HISTORICAL ROMAN COINS

21. Similar to preceding, but with anchor as symbol on reverse.

Gold. 60 sesterce piece. 3·34 grammes (51·5 grains). B.M.C. II., p. 155, No. 19.

22. Similar to No. 20, but with mark of value **XXXX**, and on reverse **ROMA**.

Gold. 40 sesterce piece. 2·23 grammes (34·5 grains). B.M.C. I., p. 27, No. 187.

23. Similar to No. 20, but with mark of value **XX**, and on reverse **ROMA**.

Gold. 20 sesterce piece. 1·12 grammes (17·2 grains). B.M.C. I., p. 27, No. 190.

24. *Obv.* Head of Roma r.; behind, **X**.

Rev. The Dioscuri on horseback charging r.; below horses, anchor; on tablet, **ROMA**.

Silver *denarius*. 4·06 grammes (62·7 grains). B.M.C. II., p. 155, No. 21.

The date of the first issue of gold from the mint at Rome is a matter of much dispute. Pliny has a definite statement to the effect that the "gold coin was first struck 51 years after the silver, the *scripulum* being equivalent to 20 *sestertii*, and the pound therefore amounting in value to 5760 *sestertii* of the time."[1] Fifty-one years from the introduction of the

---

[1] *N. H.* 33. 47. His source here is probably not the same as that whence he derived the date 217 B.C. for the uncial reduction and the equation of the *denarius* to 16 *asses* (see below, Nos. 26, 27). The passage is tacked on, at the end of the section about coinage, somewhat loosely, and looks like a note taken from some other authority. As regards the date, the good Bamberg MS. reads LI, the others LXII.

HISTORICAL ROMAN COINS

denarius bring us to 218 or 217 B.C., according as we accept the Plinian or the Livian date for the earlier reform. Now it is a principle well-known to numismatists, and evidently familiar also to ancient historians, that isolated gold coinages were usually initiated in times of monetary distress. There was no unusual strain on the Roman finances in the year 218.[1] The Senate took no steps to raise extraordinary forces for the coming opening campaign. But after the disaster of Trasimene in April, 217, all the circumstances were such as would justify the issue of a special gold coinage. We have therefore here an independent confirmation[2] of the Livian (268) as against the Plinian date (269) for the introduction of the *denarius*.

Now the date 217, to which the issue of gold coin is on this evidence assigned, has generally been accepted as correct. We have little pieces of gold of three denominations, with marks of value representing 60 (Nos. 20, 21), 40 (No. 22) and 20 (No. 23), and

---

Willers (*Corolla Numism.*, p. 314) corrects to LX, and makes the passage refer to the well-known gold Romano-Campanian coins with the oath-taking scene, which he assigns to 209 B.C. He has not made out his case; see Haeberlin in *Zeit. f. Num.* xxvi., pp. 241 f.

[1] See Mommsen, *Hist. of Rome*, or the passage from Neumann quoted by Willers, *op. cit.*, p. 312.

[2] The confirmation is not affected by the possibility that no such gold coinage was really struck in 217 B.C. We assume that Pliny's authority thought it was, and made his chronological reckoning accordingly.

equating them to as many *sestertii* respectively. The denominations weigh in scruples 3, 2 and 1 respectively. There is no reason to doubt that Pliny's authority had these coins in mind when he gave the value of the gold scruple in sesterces. Whether he is right in his date is quite another question.

Count de Salis, in his arrangement of the British Museum collection, divided our gold pieces into two classes, (1) those of poor style, with moneyers' symbols, (2) those of good style, without symbols. The latter he assigned to Rome; the others, with the corresponding *denarii* and bronze coins, he assigned to local mints; and both classes, according to his chronological classification, belong to about 240—229 B.C.

Now, what is the basis of this chronology? If we take the gold pieces which bear symbols, and which were apparently issued at local mints, we find the following symbols: anchor, spear-head, staff, pentagon, ear of corn. The same symbols occur also on *denarii* and on bronze of the sextantal standard. But those who wish to maintain the later date of the gold pieces in question point out that four out of these five symbols, viz., the anchor, the spear-head, the staff, the pentagon, occur on *denarii* or bronze coins which must, owing to the bronze being uncial in standard, be ascribed to a later date, since the uncial standard superseded the sextantal in 217 B.C. It does not, however, follow from this that the gold coins must belong to the later date, but only that we are free to make our choice between the two dates. The bulk of the evidence of the symbols points to the earlier, and so also does the style of the gold coins which, in the specimens assigned to the Roman mint by de Salis, is very much better than the style of the *denarii* which belong to the years about 217 B.C.

But if we accept de Salis's date, Pliny's statement as to the year in which gold was first struck at Rome must be rejected. That statement may indeed well have been due to some antiquary's constructive imagination. We must not, as we have already seen, be misled by Pliny's circumstantiality.[1] There is nothing more easy than to be circumstantial in support of a conjecture. An antiquary, who had made up his mind that these gold coins were issued during the great Hannibalian crisis, would very naturally reckon back to see how many years it was since the introduction of the silver coinage. The fact that Pliny specifies this number of years adds no credibility to his statement. The modern archæologist bases his date, right or wrong, on the comparison between the gold coins themselves and the other objects with which they must have been contemporary, viz., the *denarii*

[1] He is of course often demonstrably wrong, and usually muddled; but Mommsen (ii., p. 12) unnecessarily accuses him, or his and Festus's authority, Verrius Flaccus, of saying that the *quadrigati* and *bigati* were the most ancient *denarii*. The passage means no more than that the *quadrigati* and *bigati* were so called from their types.

and bronze coins, which by their weight or style are shown to belong to the period before the Hannibalian crisis.

There is no other Roman gold coinage which can reasonably be attributed to the year 217 or 218 B.C. If the theory described above is true, then either Pliny's source is untrustworthy, or Pliny himself has misunderstood his authority, or such gold coins as were then struck have disappeared.

Next let us examine de Salis's date, and see whether we can narrow its limits. His suggestion of 240—229 B.C. may be allowed to include a margin of a few years on either side. Now, in antiquity, such isolated gold coinages as we are discussing were, as we have said, almost always issued during crises. A good instance is the gold coinage struck when the Arcadians seized Olympia in 365 B.C. and placed the conduct of the games in the hands of the Pisatans.[1] The exceptional gold issues of Athens dating from 407 and 338 B.C. are well known. Recently, a group of electrum coins struck by Chios and other Ionian states has been, with great probability, ascribed to the crisis of the Ionic Revolt.[2] The types of the coins before us, be it noted, are distinctly martial. But in 240 B.C. Rome had passed through her crisis. The

---

[1] *Hist. Greek Coins*, p. 76.
[2] P. Gardner, *The Gold Coinage of Asia before Alexander the Great* in *Proc. Brit. Acad.* iii.

HISTORICAL ROMAN COINS

First Punic War was just over. The time was therefore not apt for a special coinage.

We have, however, seen that, according to the most probable chronology, the sextantal standard was legalized as early as 268 B.C. So far, therefore, as we may argue from the sextantal bronze coins with which the local issues of gold are associated, that gold coinage may date back to 268 B.C. The *denarii* with symbols, on the other hand, do not seem to be of quite the earliest type. In fact, the mere appearance of the symbol is a sign that they are likely to be comparatively late. It may be suggested, therefore, that the coinage in question belongs to the end of the First Punic War, in fact to that final crisis which immediately preceded the victory of Catulus at Aegusa (10 March, 241). We know that the fleet which won this battle was provided by private subscription. Two hundred ships manned by sixty thousand men: for such a force a special issue of coin must have been necessary. It is to this date then that we would conjecturally attribute the gold coins of 60, 40 and 20 sesterces, and the corresponding silver and bronze coins.

Such is the argument in favour of an early date for the gold pieces of 60, 40 and 20 sesterces. The arguments against it, as summarized by Dr. Haeberlin,[1]

[1] In a private communication, for which I desire to express my indebtedness.

are: (1) if it is accepted, Pliny's evidence must be rejected; (2) the fleet in 242 was raised by private efforts, not by the state; (3) it is probable that a gold issue accompanied the uncial reform of 217, gold being tariffed above its real value; and such an excessive value for gold suits no other year better than the crisis of 217; (4) the evidence from the symbols is not against the later date. With (1) and (4) we have already dealt. In reply to (2) it may be said that although the fleet was raised by voluntary efforts, money was necessary to pay the crews. Demarete voluntarily provided the treasure out of which the Demareteia were coined, but it was the state that coined them.[1] As regards (3), there was a crisis in 242, as there was in 217; though perhaps not so serious, it might easily have led to the issue of gold at a rate above its real value.

THE ACQUISITION OF CORCYRA.

229 B.C.

25. *Obv.* Head of Jupiter r., laureate.

Rev. Victory crowning a trophy; in exergue, ROMA; in the field, monograms of KOPK and ΑΓ.

Silver *victoriatus.* 2·77 grammes (42·7 grains). B.M.C. II., p. 197, No. 227.

One of the consequences of the expedition to Scodra

---

[1] *Hist. Greek Coins*, p. 38.

and the suppression of the Illyrian pirates in 229 B.C. was that Corcyra became an "ally" of Rome, under a Roman governor. This was the first step of the Romans across the Adriatic. Its importance is illustrated by the fact that on, or soon after, the acquisition of the island coins of distinctly Roman character were struck there. The monograms containing the first three or four letters of the name of Corcyra, and the first two letters of the name of a Corcyraean magistrate ('Αγήσανδρος ?)[1] are all that distinguish this *victoriatus* and a contemporary *quinarius* from the *victoriati* and *quinarii* issued at Italian mints. The monogram of the name of Corcyra is of a form actually found on local coins,[2] so that there can be no doubt as to the attribution.

We have already (p. 36) had to deal incidentally with the origin of the *victoriatus*. It is hardly necessary to say that the existence of this particular *victoriatus*, with the mint-mark of Corcyra, which could not have been issued before 229 B.C., does not prove that no *victoriati* were issued before that date. The actual course of events was probably that at a somewhat earlier period the Romans began by issuing *victoriati* from Rome itself, although they were intended, as we have seen (p. 37), for extra-Roman currency. Then, when

[1] This was the name of a Corcyraean prytanis; see F. Lenormant in *Rev. Num.*, 1868, p. 152.
[2] B.M.C. *Thessaly to Aetolia*, pp. 140 ff.

more mints were established in the peninsula, they issued *victoriati* with local mint marks, such as **L, C, B, H,** or **VB** in monogram: marks which have been assigned to Luceria, Canusium, Beneventum, Herdonea and Vibo Valentia. The Corcyra mint-mark ranks with these. It is a general rule that of two similar series of coins, one with and the other without differentiating marks, the former is the earlier, since such differentiæ are usually due to increasing complexity of organization.

AFTER TRASIMENE.
217 B.C.

26. *Obv.* Head of Roma r., in winged helmet; behind, **X.**
Rev. The Dioscuri on horseback, charging r.; below, on tablet, **ROMA**; symbol, prow r.

Silver *denarius*. 4·02 grammes (62·0 grains). B.M.C. I., p. 54, No. 448.

27. *Obv.* Head of Jupiter r., laureate; behind, **S.**
Rev. Prow r.; below, **ROMA**; above, symbol, prow r.; to r. **S.**

Bronze *semis*. 14·64 grammes (226·0 grains). B.M.C. I., p. 54, No. 454.

The reduction of the bronze *as* from the weight of two ounces to one is by general consent dated to the crisis of the Hannibalian war. Verrius Flaccus, an antiquary of the Augustan age, is the authority[1] for the statement: numerum aeris perduct[um esse ad xvi in denario lege Fla]minia minus solvendi, cu[m Hannibalis bello premere]tur populus romanus.

Pliny[2] is probably, though not certainly, quoting from the same source when he says: "When Hannibal was pressing the Romans hard, in the dictatorship of Q. Fabius Maximus, the *as* was made uncial, and it was decided that the *denarius* should exchange for 16 *asses*, the *quinarius* for eight, the *sestertius* for four. Thus the state made a gain of a half" (the *as* having been previously of the weight of two *unciae*), "but, in paying military wages one *denarius* was always given for 10 *asses*." On this stage in the development of the Roman coinage some further light is thrown by a passage of Zonaras:[3] "Hieron sent many contributions, of which the Romans accepted only the corn and a figure of Victory, although they were in such pecuniary straits that they adulterated with bronze the silver money which had hitherto been unadulterated and pure."

Another passage of Pliny relating to this same year 217, and the supposed first issue of gold money, has already been discussed (above, p. 21).

There is a contradiction between the passages of

---

[1] Apud Festum, p. 347, quoted by Mommsen-Blacas, ii., p. 11.
[2] *N. H.*, 33. 45.
[3] 8.26.

HISTORICAL ROMAN COINS

Pliny and of Festus, since, as Mommsen points out, Flaminius was dead before Fabius became dictator. If the reform was due to a *lex Flaminia*, it must have been promulgated before the battle of Trasimene. But the dictatorship of Fabius is probably, and very naturally, used to date the whole year, although he only held office for part of it.

The authorities are silent on another important change which was made in this year. The weight of the *denarius* was reduced by about one-sixth. It had previously weighed about 4·55 grammes (4 scruples); it henceforth weighed about 3·90 grammes ($3\frac{1}{3}$ scruples),[1] or $\frac{1}{84}$ of a pound instead of $\frac{1}{72}$. *Denarii* of about this weight (No. 26) are associated with the uncial *as* and its divisions, such as the *semis* (No. 27). It will be noticed that the two coins illustrated have the same differentia, a prow. Since the *denarius* now weighed $\frac{1}{84}$ of the pound and was, as we are told, the equivalent of 16 *asses* of uncial weight, it follows that $\frac{1}{84}$ lb. of silver was the equivalent of $\frac{16}{12}$ lb. of bronze, so that the relation of silver to bronze was 112 : 1.[2]

The annual stipendium of the soldier was 1200 *asses*. For this he continued to receive 120 *denarii*, and not 75 only, as he would have done had he been

---

[1] It is significant that this is the weight of the Carthaginian drachm. Haeberlin, *Metrolog. Grundlagen*, p. 61, note.

[2] $\frac{16}{12} \times 84 = 112$.

subjected to the new rate. Later, Julius Cæsar trebled the number of *asses* in the stipendium, giving 3600 instead of 1200; but he reckoned these *asses* at the modern rate of 16 to the *denarius*, so that he paid his soldiers 225 *denarii* a year.[1]

The fact that in 217 B.C. the number of *asses* for which a *denarius* was given, in estimating the pay of the Roman legionary, remained unchanged, is supposed to account for the retention of the mark of value **X**. That mark, indeed, was probably by this time regarded as denoting the name rather than the value of the coin. The numerals **XVI** appear for a short time on *denarii* which may be dated about 140 B.C.[2] Still later (about 125), the form ✳ appears, and becomes usual. This does not mean **XVI**, as some have supposed, but is merely **X** differentiated as denominational mark by means of a horizontal stroke. The stroke was more often, in such cases, placed above the letter; but a passage of Maecianus[3] confirms the explanation just given, for besides the form ✳ for *denarius* he gives a **V** similarly erased as the mark of the *quinarius*. The *quinarius* was not issued again until the end of the second century; when it reappeared, it was marked with a **Q**.

---

[1] Tac. *Ann.*, i., 17.
[2] Grueber, B.M.C., *Rom. Rep.*, i., p. 118.
[3] Hultsch, *Metrol. Script.*, ii., p. 66.

HISTORICAL ROMAN COINS

HANNIBAL IN CAPUA.
216—215 B.C.

28. *Obv.* Janiform head of Persephone, wearing corn-wreath.

Rev. Jupiter in quadriga r., driven by Victory; he holds sceptre in l. and wields thunderbolt in r.

Electrum. 2·79 grammes (43·0 grains). B.M.C. II., p. 139, No. 147.

The attribution of these coins, as regards date and mint, is more or less conjectural; but the conjecture[1] has been generally accepted. The types, on the obverse recalling, on the reverse actually repeating, the types of the *quadrigati* (see No. 10), identify the mint, without possibility of reasonable doubt, as Capua. But instead of the beardless head of Janus, we have a janiform head of a divinity wearing a wreath of corn-ears, in which every person acquainted with the coins of Carthage will recognize a janiform representation of the goddess Persephone, as the artists of the later Carthaginian issues conceived her. She is made janiform in order to appeal as familiar to the Campanians who had long used the *quadrigati*. These very Campanians had been accustomed to good honest gold, silver and bronze; electrum now made its first appearance in Italy. The Carthaginians had for some

---

[1] Due chiefly to Percy Gardner, *Num. Chron.* 1884, pp. 220 f.

time been issuing coins in this somewhat unsatisfactory mixture, an expedient to which they had been driven by the gradual loss of their wealthy possessions in Sicily and Spain. Finally, the weight is peculiar; the maximum seems to be 3·10 grammes (47·9 grains). Now that is very close to the weight of the Carthaginian electrum coins of the period 218—146 B.C.[1] The conclusion is irresistible that we have here Carthaginian coins struck at a Campanian mint, which is tantamount to saying that they were issued when Hannibal was in possession of Capua. They illustrate the Punic art of slily adapting the coinage of their neighbours, with slight modifications, an art which is vividly displayed in the case of the earliest Siculo-Punic coinage.[2]

M. AEMILIUS LEPIDUS AND PTOLEMAEUS V.

201 B.C.

29. *Obv.* Head of the City of Alexandria (**ALEXAN-DREA**) r., wearing turreted crown.

   Rev. M. Aemilius Lepidus placing a wreath on the head of Ptolemaeus V., who holds a sceptre; inscription, **M·LEPIDVS TVTOR**

---

[1] L. Müller, *Num. de l'anc. Afrique*, ii., p. 86, Nos. 70—73; max. 3·05 grammes (47·1 grains).
[2] Hill, *Coins of Ancient Sicily*, Pl. X.

HISTORICAL ROMAN COINS

REG·PONF·MAX·S·C· (the NF ligatured to represent NTIF).

Silver *denarius*. 3·98 grammes (61·5 grains). B.M.C. I., p. 449, No. 3648.

This coin was struck about 65 B.C. by M. Aemilius Lepidus, a descendant of the person whom it commemorates. Other coins of the same date and moneyer represent (1) the equestrian statue, granted by the Senate, of one Aemilius Lepidus, who as a boy of fifteen slew an enemy in battle and saved the life of a Roman citizen; (2) the Basilica Aemilia. The inscription on the former is M·LEPIDVS AN·XV· PR·H·O·C·S· Valerius Maximus tells the story, and uses the phrase *progressus in aciem*. Consequently the abbreviations have been resolved: an(norum) XV. pr(ogressus) h(ostem) o(ccisit) c(ivem) s(ervavit). But the participle *progressus* can hardly be used absolutely.[1] A better suggestion is *praetextatus*, although his standing is sufficiently indicated by AN·XV.[2] It seems to be generally assumed, without

---

[1] Mr. George Macdonald suggests that, in view of the extraordinary coincidence between the words of Valerius Maximus (*progressus in aciem hostem interemit, civem servavit*) and the inscription on the coin, *progressus* may after all be right; Valerius Maximus, or his authority, may be quoting (from memory) the actual inscription of which the coin gives a shorthand version. But these abbreviated inscriptions on Roman coins show a curious conscientiousness on the part of the engravers, who represent every word of the original in some way (cf. No. 96).

[2] There is no stop between the P and the R, otherwise P(opuli) R(omani), qualifying H(ostem), would be possible.

any evidence, that this youthful hero was the man
who is represented on No. 29 as "tutor" of the
young Egyptian King. As regards the Basilica
Aemilia, that was built by the propraetor M. Aemilius
Lepidus out of the plunder which he accumulated
during his governorship of Sicily in 80 B.C. The
moneyer was probably the son of this propraetor.

The man with whom we are at present concerned was
despatched in 201 B.C. with two others (who, though
older than he, played a subordinate part throughout)
to Egypt and Syria, in order to secure the support of
their rulers against Philip V.[1] At the time,
Ptolemaeus V. was a minor, and two writers, not
indeed of the highest authority, seem to confirm the
statement of the coin that Aemilius acted as the
king's guardian. Valerius Maximus[2] tells us that
Ptolemaeus IV. had by his will appointed the Roman
people guardians of his son, and that the Senate
despatched as its representatives three men, including
M. Aemilius Lepidus, Pontifex Maximus and twice
consul.[3] Further, Justin confirms the statement about

---

[1] Polybius xvi. 27. 5; Liv. xxxi. 2. 3.
[2] VI. 6. 1.
[3] Niese, *Gesch. d. gr. u. mak. St.* ii., p. 637 note, argues that this description implies a later date, since Lepidus was not consul II. until 175 B.C. He might have added that he was not pontifex maximus until 180 B.C. It is more surprising to find that even by Mommsen-Blacas (ii., p. 501, note) Valerius is also accused of a "faute de chronologie." Obviously the titles "twice consul" and "pontifex maximus" are only used by Valerius, as by the designer

the will of Ptolemaeus IV.,[1] and says that the Alexandrians demanded a regent from the Romans, who were only too glad of this excuse for interference.[2] A third writer, who commands more respect, Tacitus,[3] also reminds his readers that "maiores M. Lepidum Ptolemaei liberis tutorem in Aegyptum miserant." There was, then, certainly a very distinct belief, as early as the period of our *denarius*, *i.e.*, about 65 B.C., that the mission of Aemilius to Egypt was prompted by the demand, expressed either by Ptolemaeus IV. or by the Alexandrians, for the interference of Rome. Now, modern criticism[4] has discovered that there is "no room" for a Roman guardian of the king at this period. Of guardians the little Ptolemaeus has first Agathokles, then Tlepolemos, and then Aristomenes. Also, Polybius and Livy say nothing about such a function being fulfilled by Aemilius. In any case, he left Egypt very soon, for we hear of him anywhere rather than in that country. It seems, however, unnecessary to conclude that the story of the guardianship is entirely a myth of comparatively late origin. Whether the will of Ptolemaeus IV. appointed

of the coin, to distinguish this Aemilius from others, not with chronological significance.

[1] XXXI. i. 2.
[2] XXX. ii. 8; iii. 3 f. Mittitur et M. Lepidus in Aegyptum, qui tutorio nomine regnum pupilli administret.
[3] *Annal.* ii. 67.
[4] See Niese, *loc. cit.*, and Svoronos, *Münzen der Ptol.*, IV. 260 ff.

HISTORICAL ROMAN COINS

Rome the guardian of his son or not, we can well imagine that the Romans would take full advantage of any claim, real or invented, to such a title. It might be used diplomatically, and yet not find a place in the narrative of a Polybius or a Livy. It seems reasonable, therefore, to believe that the story of this guardianship is founded upon fact, although some elements of exaggeration may have made their way into the family tradition.

Count de Salis attributed the coin with which we are dealing to the year 65 B.C., approximately. The date is based on the stylistic connexion between this moneyer's coins and the coins of Q. Pomponius Musa and M. Piso M. f. Frugi, which de Salis assigns, on different grounds, to 67 and 66 B.C. respectively. Mommsen, on the other hand, prefers the date 61, since about that time negotiations, upon which the fate of Egypt hung, were going on at Rome. There is, it is true, no reason to assume that the type must have been inspired by some event of the moment; it was chosen primarily as an illustration of the moneyer's family history. Nevertheless, there may well have been some such connexion with current events. We know that Ptolemaeus Auletes spent the greater part of his reign and much of his fortune in attempts to obtain the support of Rome. Some circumstances in his intrigues even as early as 65 B.C. may therefore well have inspired the type.

HISTORICAL ROMAN COINS

The *denarius* which we have been discussing bears neither the word **ROMA** nor those types which were characteristic of this class of coin in its first stages. In our next section we shall see how the original character of the *denarius* was gradually modified during the second century. Both these modifications, and the disappearance, at a still later date, of the word **ROMA**, seem to have been due to the same ultimate cause, viz., the gradual development of the *denarius* into a world-currency, and the elimination of its rivals.[1]

CHANGES IN THE DENARIUS.
SECOND CENTURY B.C.

30. *Obv.* Head of Roma r., in winged helmet; behind, **X**

  Rev. Luna, with crescent on forehead, in chariot r. drawn by two galloping horses; below, a prawn, and (on tablet) **ROMA**.

Silver *denarius*. 3·95 grammes (60·9 grains). B.M.C. I., p. 75, No. 585.

31. *Obv.* Similar to No. 30.

  Rev. Victory, winged, in chariot r. drawn by two galloping horses; below, **V·SAVF** (the **VF** ligatured) and **ROMA** (on tablet).

Silver *denarius*. 4·06 grammes (62·7 grains). B.M.C. I., p. 111, No. 834

---

[1] See Macdonald, *Coin Types*, p. 185.

HISTORICAL ROMAN COINS

32. *Obv.* Similar to No. 30, but behind the head a one-handled jug.

   Rev. She-wolf suckling the twins Romulus and Remus; in the background the ruminal fig-tree with birds perched on it; on the l. the shepherd Faustulus leaning on staff and raising r. hand; around, **SEX·ΓOM· [FO]STLVS**; in exergue, **ROMA**.

Silver *denarius*. 3·89 grammes (60·0 grains). B.M.C. I., p. 132, No. 927.

These three pieces serve well to illustrate the character of the changes through which the *denarius* passed in the first three quarters of the second century. No. 30, according to de Salis's classification, belongs to the period 196—173 B.C.; No. 31 to the period 172—151; and No. 32 to the period 150—125. The definitions of these periods are, it must be remembered, somewhat conjectural; but it may be taken as certain that all three coins belong to the first 75 years of the century, and that they are arranged, relatively to each other, in chronological order.

The reverse of No. 30 gives us the earliest variation from the original *denarius* type of the Dioscuri. The goddess is generally described as Diana; sometimes as "Diana or Luna." It is, however, preferable to distinguish her as Luna. The two deities were for long kept distinct; and Diana, as worshipped at Rome in early times, was the Latin goddess of the type known in the famous sanctuary of Aricia. She was essentially the goddess of childbirth and the helper of women. It is doubtful whether she would be represented as the goddess is represented on our coin, although figures of the Diana Nemorensis from Nemi do represent her, owing to Greek influence, as a huntress. If we could suppose the coin-type to be meant for the Romano-Greek Diana-Artemis, we should have an interesting historical combination, accounting for her appearance on the coins at this time. For in 187 B.C. the consul M. Aemilius Lepidus, during his campaign against the Ligurians, vowed a temple to Diana, which he dedicated during his censorship in 179.[1] But it is probable that the Greek Artemis would also have been represented as the huntress-goddess, even as we find her on the coins issued at Syracuse just before this period, during the democracy of 215—212 B.C. The goddess on our coins is so evidently characterized as Luna or the Moon that we have no justification for calling her anything else.

Now this goddess was much revered at Rome. Her chief temple, said to have been founded by Servius Tullius,[2] lay on the slope of the Aventine,

[1] Liv. xxxix. 2, xl. 52. This, and a temple of Iuno Regina, dedicated at the same time, were in the neighbourhood of the Circus Flaminius.

[2] Ovid, *Fast.* iii. 883 ; Tac. *Ann.* xv. 41. In 182 B.C. a storm forem ex aede Lunae, quae in Aventino est, raptam tulit, et in posticis partibus Cereris templi affixit (Liv. xl. 2).

ad circum maximum. The other shrines, such as that of Noctiluca on the Palatine,[1] seem to have been less important. Was there any historical reason for the adoption of the moon-goddess as a coin-type during the period to which these coins are attributed? The only event which seems to suggest itself is the reform of the calendar which took place, by the provisions of the *lex Acilia*, in the year 191 B.C. The calendar[2] had fallen into serious confusion in the year 207 B.C., when the principle of intercalation was given up. Apparently it was thought that the sun-god Apollo was offended because the expression in the calendar of his annual course was distorted by contamination with the foreign lunar element. So the intercalary month was dropped, and it was not until the year 191 that the consul M' Acilius Glabrio effected a reform. The details of this may not be quite certain, but there is no doubt that it had to do with the restoration of something like the old system. The moon, therefore, may be regarded as having come to her own again, and it is hardly fanciful to conjecture that such a change may have been commemorated by the introduction of the type of Luna into the coinage. If so, we may date the first appearance of these coins to the year of the consulship of Acilius, 191 B.C.

[1] Hor. *Carm*. iv. 6. 38.
[2] For an account of this episode, see Unger, *Zeitrechnung*, in Iwan Müller's *Handbuch*, i^2. pp. 804 f.

HISTORICAL ROMAN COINS

The coin of L. Saufeius bears the device of Victory in a biga, another of the types which helped to break down the monopoly of the Dioscuri. It is probably to coins like this and the preceding that Tacitus refers when he alludes to the popularity among the northern barbarians of the coins bearing a biga.[1]

If we seek a motive for the adoption in the period 172—151 of Victory as a new type for the *denarius* we may find it in the signal successes which in this period attended the Roman arms. The crushing defeat of Antiochus the Great at Magnesia in 190 B.C. had placed the whole of the Levant virtually at the feet of Rome. But even more striking, because much nearer home, was the victory at Pydna in 168—that final humiliation of the Greeks which allowed Rome to enter upon the inheritance of Alexander the Great. It is not surprising that such a change in her position should be reflected in the coinage.

The type of Sex. Pompeius Fostlus, on the other hand, is one of those personal types which began to appear once it was felt that change in the reverse type of the *denarius* was permissible. The process is characteristic of Roman historical development: first, complete uniformity; then the beginnings of change,

---

[1] *Germ.* 5 : *pecuniam probant veterem et diu notam, serratos bigatosque.* The *serrati* are the coins with notched or serrated edges, regarding which see No. 47.

HISTORICAL ROMAN COINS

but still without the obvious intrusion of the personal element; finally, the domination of the individual.[1]

Behind the wolf and twins stands the *ficus ruminalis*, which once shaded the Lupercal, or cave in which Romulus and Remus were suckled by the she-wolf. Of the birds, which on good specimens may be made out on the tree, one should be the *picus Martis*, the woodpecker sacred to Mars.[2] The type is either merely a "canting" type, referring to the cognomen of the moneyer Sex. Pompeius (or Pomponius) Fostlus,[3] or else, as is more probable, it indicates a claim on his part to be descended from Faustulus, the shepherd who rescued the twins. In any case, the reference of the type is strictly personal. The one-handled vase which occurs as a symbol on all the coins of this moneyer, irrespective of their type, has been explained, presumably in jest, as a milk-jug, because the she-wolf is giving her milk to the twins.[4]

The initials of the moneyers began to be placed on the coins during the period 217—197 B.C. It was

---

[1] See Mommsen-Blacas, ii., p. 43, and Macdonald, *Coin Types*, pp. 190 f.

[2] On most other representations (*e.g.*, the gems in Bötticher, *Baumkultus*, fig. 37; Furtwängler, *Antike Gemmen*, Pl. xxviii., 58) only one bird is to be seen; on the Bolsena mirror (*Mon. dell' Instituto*, xi., Pl. 3. 1) there appear an owl and a woodpecker.

[3] Roman moneyers were very fond of "canting" types. See Macdonald, *Coin Types*, p. 188.

[4] Babelon, *Monn. de la Rép. Romaine*, ii., p. 336; by Mommsen-Blacas, ii., p. 503, the vase is also described as a milk-jug.

about this time, it would seem, that the consuls lost the right of coinage within the city. Consequently the special board of magistrates, *tresviri monetales*, appointed from time to time when money was needed, naturally began to leave their mark on the coinage. We find first of all only symbols, then initials, then abbreviations of a less scanty kind, and finally a full indication of the moneyer's name.

C. MINUCIUS AUGURINUS.
CIRCA 150—125 B.C.

33. *Obv.* Head of Roma r., wearing winged helmet; under chin, X; behind, ROMA.

Rev. Corinthian column, supporting a figure of L. Minucius Augurinus, resting on staff and holding ears of corn (?); from the capital hang bells; at the base, lions' heads surmounted by ears of corn; on r., M. Minucius Faesus standing, togate, holding a lituus; on l., L. (or P.) Minucius Augurinus standing, togate, holding a dish and a loaf, his l. foot resting on a corn measure;[1] above, C·AVG.

Silver *denarius*, 3·86 grammes (59·5 grains). B.M.C. I., p. 136, No. 953.

A. B. Cook, *J. H. S.* xxii., p. 19, describes him as clapping cymbals, with his foot on a ball. But his left hand and right hand hold the objects differently.

HISTORICAL ROMAN COINS

The popular hero of the Minucia gens was L. Minucius Augurinus, who as *praefectus annonae* in 439 B.C., when there was a serious famine, obtained a supply of corn from abroad, and in three market days lowered the price of corn to a maximum of one *as* for a modius. The grateful people erected to him a brazen statue on a column outside the Porta Trigemina, everyone subscribing an *uncia*.[1] The column, with the statue on it, is represented on the coin. The two figures at the sides of the monument have been explained as other members of the family. The man on the right, holding the augur's wand, may then be M. Minucius Faesus, one of the first plebeian augurs to be elected after the passing of the *lex Ogulnia* in 300 B.C.[2] The man on the left may be either the *praefectus annonae* himself—admiring his own monument—or P. Minucius Augurinus, a still earlier public benefactor, who as consul in 492 B.C. relieved a famine by obtaining supplies from abroad.[3] But it is quite possible that the augur on the right is merely a canting allusion to the moneyer's cognomen, while the figure on the left may also have some allusive significance which escapes us.

The ears of corn flanking the monument need no

---

[1] Plin. *N. H.* xviii. 4; xxxiv. 11. This, Pliny thinks, was perhaps the first honour of the kind conferred by the people, not by the Senate. Cp. Dion. Hal. περὶ ἐπιβουλῶν, p. xxxvi, ed. C. Mueller.

[2] Liv. x. 9.

[3] Liv. ii. 34.

explanation. The lions' heads may be either purely ornamental or apotropaic; less probably they were fountains. The bells are difficult to explain. It has been thought that they were used to announce the opening and closing of the corn market;[1] but what possible market was held outside the Porta Trigemina, which led through the walls below the north-west slope of the Aventine, close to the Tiber? Like the bells on the *façade* of the second temple of Jupiter Capitolinus, they were probably prophylactic,[2] though why they should be used here we cannot say. It is, however, significant that one of the most important rites performed by the augurs was *augurare vineta virgetaque*, apparently with the object of protecting the crops in general from damage by drought.[3] Bells may have played some part in this ceremony.[4]

This coin is attributed to the third quarter of the second century. A certain C. Minucius Augurinus,

---

[1] Babelon, ii., p. 228.
[2] A. B. Cook in *J. H. S.*, *loc. cit.*
[3] Wissowa in Pauly-Wissowa, *Realencycl.*, ii. 2329.
[4] The bells and the lions' heads recall the *Dípon* or *Díwat*, a granite pillar at Mahoba in India. "Its name is derived from the practice of placing a lamp, or *díp*, on its summit on stated occasions. But this certainly could not have been the original purpose of the pillar, as it is crowned with a broad, flat-topped capital, and does not possess a single receptacle for a lamp. It is a single shaft 18 ft. in height . . . the uppermost (portion) is ornamented with four chains, and bells suspended from four lions' heads immediately beneath the capital." Alex. Cunningham, *Archæol. Survey of India, Reports*, Vol. ii. (1871), p. 443.

perhaps the moneyer's father, was tribune of the plebs in 187 B.C. The Ti. Minucius C. f. Augurinus, who a little later struck coins with a very similar representation of the ancestral monument, was doubtless the son of our Caius.

T. QUINCTIUS FLAMININUS.
CIRCA 124—103 B.C.

34. *Obv.* Head of Roma r., in winged helmet; behind, flamen's *apex ;* under chin, ✷.
Rev. The Dioscuri on horseback, charging r. ; below, **TQ** and round Macedonian shield; in exergue, **ROMA**.

Silver *denarius.* 3·88 grammes (59·8 grains). B.M.C. I., p. 155, No. 1040.

The moneyer who issued this *denarius*—which is dated by some to a slightly earlier period—must have been a descendant of T. Quinctius Flamininus, who won the battle of Cynoscephalae in 197 B.C., since the letters **TQ** on the reverse, combined with the *flamen's* cap on the obverse, clearly represent a person of this name, while the Macedonian shield indicates a Macedonian victory, as on the coins of M. Caecilius Metellus.[1]

This being so, we can see a special significance in the use of the type of the Dioscuri here, for it was at this time no longer the ordinary type of the *denarius*, and we know that the conqueror of Philip V. made a

---
[1] Babelon, i., p. 269.

special dedication to the Dioscuri at Delphi. The objects dedicated were silver bucklers (ἀσπίδας) and his own *scutum* (τὸν ἑαυτοῦ θυρεόν).[1] The bucklers were doubtless Macedonian bucklers, one of which is represented on the coin under the figures of the Ζηνὸς κραιπναῖσι γεγαθότες ἱπποσύναισι κοῦροι, to whom it was dedicated.

Which of Flamininus' descendants issued this coin we do not know. It is usually ascribed to the one who became consul in 123 B.C., in which case it must have been issued some time before that date, since the office of moneyer was of comparatively low rank. The date here adopted—on grounds of style—is due to Count de Salis.

CHARTERS OF LIBERTY.

35. *Obv.* Head of Roma r. in winged helmet; under chin, ✵ ; behind, **LAECA**.

Rev. Libertas, crowned by Victory, in fast quadriga to r., holding cap of Liberty and sceptre; below, **M·ΠORC**; in exergue, **ROMA**.

Silver *denarius*. 3·98 grammes (61·5 grains). B.M.C. I., p. 151, No. 1024.

36. *Obv.* Head of Roma r. in winged helmet; above, **ROMA**; in front, **X**; behind, **P·LAECA** (the **AE** in monogram).

[1] Plut. *Titus*, 12.

Rev. A general wearing a cuirass and armed with a sword, accompanied by a lictor holding in his right hand a long stake[1] or spear erect, in his left, two rods (the fasces). The general extends his hand over the head of a togate figure; below, PROVOCO.

Silver *denarius.* 3·90 grammes (60·2 grains). British Museum.

37. *Obv.* Head of Roma r. in winged helmet; behind, ✷ and voting urn (*sitella*).

Rev. Libertas in fast quadriga r., holding cap of Liberty and sceptre; below, C·CASSI; in exergue, ROMA.

Silver *denarius.* 3·89 grammes (60·0 grains). B.M.C. I., p. 153, No. 1033.

38. *Obv.* Head of Vesta r., veiled; behind, Q.CASSIVS; before, VEST.

Rev. Circular temple of Vesta, surmounted by a figure of the goddess, holding sceptre and patera; within, curule chair; on l., urn (*sitella*); on r., tablet (*sorticula*) inscribed A C.

Silver *denarius.* 3·98 grammes (61·5 grains). B.M.C. I., p. 482, No. 3871.

39. *Obv.* Head of Vesta l. veiled; behind, two-handled cup; before, letter A.

---

[1] This suggestion is due to Mr. Stuart Jones, who thinks it may be meant for the stake to which criminals were tied for flogging. It is however very slight in form and might even be a long sword.

HISTORICAL ROMAN COINS

Rev. A citizen, togate, dropping into a cista a tablet inscribed V; behind him, **LONGIN IIIV**.

Silver *denarius*. 3·89 grammes (60·0 grains). B.M.C. I., p. 494, No. 3929.

The allusions on the reverses of Nos. 35, 36 are to an ancestor or ancestors of the moneyers, who carried the laws *pro tergo civium*, which were among the chief charters of the people's liberty.[1] Nothing is known of the moneyers themselves; but the first coin and the third appear to belong to the same period, and that the end of the second century B.C. The second moneyer (No. 36) probably issued his coins from one of the local Italian mints about 90 B.C. His coin is supposed to allude to the extension of the right of *provocatio* even against military commanders: in the general is seen a provincial governor from whom the *ius in capita civium* was taken away by one of the three Porcian laws. The gesture of the general, then, is not one of protection, as we should naturally suppose.

---

[1] Liv. x. 9; Cic. *pro. Rab. perd.* 4 (12); cp. *in Verr.* ii., 5. 63 (163); *de Rep.* ii. 31: leges Porciae, quae tres sunt trium Porciorum. The dates of these laws are uncertain; one was before the time of the Gracchi, another was suggested by Cato the Elder (Festus s.v. *Pro Scapulis*). See Mommsen-Blacas, ii., p. 321. One of these Leges Porciae authorized appeal to the people from the holder of the military imperium; this was before 108 B.C., for a statement of Sallust (*Bell. Jug.* 69) proves that at that date the commander had the right against the Latins but not against the Romans: Turpilius . . . iussus a Metello causam dicere, postquam sese parum expurgat, condemnatus verberatusque capite poenas solvit; nam is civis ex Latio erat.

HISTORICAL ROMAN COINS

Of the three Cassian coins, No. 37 is generally attributed to C. Cassius Longinus, son of L. Cassius Longinus Ravilla. No. 38 is given to Q. Cassius Longinus, quaestor to Pompeius in Spain in 54 B.C., and notorious for his harsh treatment of the provincials. His coinage probably dates from about 58 B.C. The third, No. 39, probably belongs to L. Cassius Longinus, who seems to have been triumvir of the mint about 52 B.C.

It was Ravilla who, in 137 B.C., as tribune of the plebs, carried the second *lex tabellaria*, extending the process of voting by ballot to the public tribunals; it had been introduced two years before for the elections of magistrates. He it was also who, when the decision of the Pontifex, Lucius Metellus, in the trial of the Vestal Virgins in 113 B.C., was regarded as too lenient, was appointed president of the commission to re-hear the case. The *lex tabellaria* was one of the most popular of democratic measures, and Ravilla was therefore regarded as an especial champion of liberty. That is why Libertas figures on the coinage of his son.[1] The voting urn on the obverse, however, refers not to this reform, but to Ravilla's action in the affair of the Vestals. The same is the case with the urn and the voting tablet with the letters **AC** (*absolvo, condemno*)

---

[1] C. Cassius must have been moneyer at the latest about 104 B.C. (he was consul in 96), so that the events alluded to on his coins were very recent.

on the coin of Q. Cassius (No. 38); and the curule chair within the temple is the chair of the judge. The method of voting, by placing tablets indicating acquittal or condemnation in an urn, was employed in *quaestiones*, such as that which was concerned with the Vestals. But in the comitia, when the people were voting on a rogation, the tablets bore or indicated the words *antiquo* and *uti rogas*. Mommsen adds[1] that in the comitia the tablets were placed not in an urn, but in a *cista* or box; and this method is illustrated on the coin of L. Cassius Longinus (No. 39). Here is a citizen voting, according to the *lex tabellaria* of Cassius Ravilla; and in favour of the proposal before the comitia, since his tablet bears the letter **V** for *uti rogas*.

THE SURRENDER OF JUGURTHA BY BOCCHUS.
106 OR 105 B.C.

40. *Obv.* Bust of Diana r., wearing stephane, with crescent above; behind, lituus; in front, **FAVSTVS**.

Rev. Sulla seated l. on a platform; before him, kneeling r., Bocchus holding up an olive branch; behind him, Jugurtha kneeling l., his hands tied behind his back; above, on r., **FELIX**.

Silver *denarius*. 3·87 grammes (59·7 grains). B.M.C. I., p. 471, No. 3824.

[1] Mommsen-Blacas, ii., p. 504, note.

HISTORICAL ROMAN COINS

This coin was struck, probably about 62 B.C., by Faustus Cornelius Sulla, son of the dictator by his fourth wife, Caecilia Metella. The story of the capture of Jugurtha is in all the history books. The interest of the type is that it probably reproduces more or less exactly the subject of a seal ring which Sulla, in his pride, had made for himself, and used constantly, much to the irritation of Marius.[1] Bocchus himself also dedicated in the temple of Capitoline Jupiter some figures of Victory bearing trophies and beside them a group in gold of the handing over of Jugurtha to Sulla.[2] The head of Diana on the obverse of our coin alludes to the dictator's especial cult of the goddess,[3] the lituus to his augurship.

The dictator is identified by the title **FELIX**, a title which he did not finally adopt until after the death of the younger Marius.[4] Faustus, therefore, on his coin commits a " chronological error " like that of which some critics have complained in connexion with the coins of M. Aemilius Lepidus.[5]

---

[1] Plut. *Sulla*, 3: ἦν δὲ ἡ γραφὴ Βόκχος μὲν παραδιδούς, Σύλλας δὲ παραλαμβάνων τὸν Ἰογόρθαν. Id. *Mar.* 10; *Praec. ger. reip.* xii.; Plin. *N. H.* xxxvii. 4. 9; Val. Max. viii. 14. 4 (*Rom.*).

[2] Plut. *Mar.* 32; *Sulla*, 6.

[3] Vell. Paterc. ii. 25: privileges granted after Sulla's victory over Norbanus to the shrine of Diana Tifatina near Capua. See also the inscriptions cited by Wissowa in Pauly-Wissowa, *Realencycl.* v. 327.

[4] Vell. Paterc. ii. 27.

[5] See *supra*, p. 53.

HISTORICAL ROMAN COINS

MARIUS AND THE BARBARIANS.

104—101 B.C.

41. *Obv.* Head of Apollo r., laureate ; behind, C·EGNATVLEI·C·F·; below, Q (NAT and VL ligatured).

Rev. Victory standing l., writing on oval shield, which is fastened to a trophy, on which are a helmet with bull's horns, cuirass and spear ; at the foot of the trophy is a war trumpet (*karnyx*) ; in the field, Q ; in the exergue, ROMA.

Silver *quinarius*. 1·85 grammes (28·5 grains). B.M.C. I., p. 165, No. 1077.

42. *Obv.* Head of Jupiter r., laureate ; under chin, ·B·

Rev. Victory standing r., holding palm branch and wreath which she is about to place on trophy ; at foot of trophy, a seated captive and a *karnyx;* in field, downwards, T·CLOVLI (VL ligatured) ; in exergue, Q.

Silver *quinarius*. 1·83 grammes (28·3 grains). B.M.C. I., p. 168, No. 1105.

The *quinarius* had fallen into disuse before the end of the third century ; it was revived by the *lex Clodia*. Pliny tells us :[1] Is qui nunc victoriatus appellatur lege Clodia percussus est. antea enim hic nummus ex Illyrico advectus mercis loco habebatur. est autem

[1] *N. H.* xxxiii. 3. 46.

signatus Victoria et inde nomen. These *victoriati* were not the coins originally so-called, but new *quinarii* with somewhat similar types. Pliny's remark about Illyricum is generally admitted to be a blunder. He confounds the Roman victoriate with the Illyrian coin of the same value.[1]

The date of the *lex Clodia* is conjectural. *Quinarii* of the new sort were struck by M. Cato, who died in 91 B.C., and the similar pieces of T. Cloulius (No. 42), C. Fundanius, C. Egnatuleius (No. 41), and P. Sabinus are older still.[2] The law is generally assigned to about 104 B.C. The coins with which we are at present concerned doubtless belong to the period immediately following the enactment, for there are none older in style. The types of the reverses evidently allude to a victory over some northern barbarians, since the horned helmet,[3] the shield, and the war trumpet are of northern, apparently Keltic, type; the last being particularly associated with the Kelts. The barbarians in question can hardly be other than some of those defeated by Marius at Aquae Sextiae or at Vercellae. At the former battle the tribes concerned were the Teutons—generally regarded as Germans—and the Ambrones, a Gallic tribe. The Cimbri, who were crushed at Vercellae,

---

[1] Mommsen-Blacas, ii., p. 87, note 2.
[2] Id. ii., p. 101.
[3] See Mowat in *Gazette archéologique*, 1887, p. 130.

have been claimed both as Kelts and as Germans; among the ancients the evidence of most of the earlier writers is in favour of their Keltic origin, while later authors (who knew the Germans better) called them Germans. But even if the Cimbri were Germans, we know so little about German armour at this date that it would be rash to deny that the Cimbri may have employed armour and trumpets such as are represented on our coins. It is therefore impossible to determine whether the reference is to a victory over any one particular tribe; and, indeed, it is most reasonable to assume that the reference is quite general to the victories over the northern barbarians; accuracy in distinguishing the armour of the various foes of Rome is hardly to be demanded of a die engraver. De Salis assigned the coins to the years 102 and 101; the latter date seems on the whole the more probable.

The letter **Q** is generally explained as a mark of value (for *quinarius*). The value of this coin, it must be remembered, was now 8 *asses*, and could no longer be strictly expressed by **V**, as on the earliest issue. Had the **Q** only occurred on the obverse, in close connexion with the name of the moneyer—as a matter of fact it is separated from the name—we should have been justified in explaining it as *Quaestor*,[1] and in supposing that Egnatuleius, for

---

[1] So Lenormant, *La Monn. dans l'ant.* ii., p. 293.

instance, was one of Marius's quaestors, who struck coins for use in the Gallic war. But the nearly, if not quite, contemporary *quinarii* of T. Cloulius all have **Q** on the reverse only, and on the obverse a series of letters differentiating the various issues.

These letters are a striking proof of the enormous quantity of dies which must have been used, for it appears that each letter marks a different die. That is to say, it is not to be supposed that, after a number of coins had been struck from a die bearing the letter **B**, that letter was erased and another engraved on the same die. A complete new die, marked with the next letter, **C**, was engraved. There are three series of these letters in the coinage of Cloulius, according as the letters are placed behind, below, or in front of the neck of Jupiter; in each series the whole alphabet is represented; and finally, the varieties are multiplied by placing dots at the sides of, below or above the letters. In the British Museum Catalogue alone Mr. Grueber enumerates 33 varieties of this *quinarius* coinage.

C. COELIUS CALDUS.

HIS ACHIEVEMENTS, 107—94 B.C.

43. *Obv.* Head, r., of C. Coelius Caldus; behind, a tablet with the letters **L. D.**; inscr. **C·COEL·CALDVS·COS.**

Rev. Head of Sol r., radiate; in front, circular shield; behind, oblong shield with thunderbolt device; inscr. **CALDVS, III·VIR.**

Silver *denarius.* 3·97 grammes (61·3 grains). B.M.C. I., p. 474, No. 3833.

44. *Obv.* Similar head and inscription; behind, a vexillum inscribed **HIS**; in front, a standard in the form of a boar.

Rev. An *epulo* preparing a *lectisternium;* at either end of the couch, a trophy, one with circular, the other with oblong shield; inscr. **L·CALDVS·VII·VIR·EPVL· C·CALDVS·IMP·A·X,** and **CALDVS III· VIR** (various ligatures).

Silver *denarius.* 4·15 grammes (64·1 grains). B.M.C. I., p. 475, No. 387.

The descendants of C. Coelius Caldus were extremely proud of their ancestor, the *homo novus* to whom the honourable position of the family in the last century of the Republic was due. These coins were struck by C. Coelius Caldus, his grandson; their precise date is uncertain, some (as Mommsen) giving them to about 54 B.C., while de Salis prefers 61 B.C. The moneyer, as one of the monetary triumvirate, signs his coins *Caldus IIIvir.*

The elder C. Coelius Caldus was tribune of the plebs in 106 B.C. In this capacity he impeached

HISTORICAL ROMAN COINS

C. Popilius Laenas, who, when the consul Cassius Longinus, the year before, had been defeated and killed by the Tigurini, came to terms with the enemy and brought off the army, with the loss of their baggage and their honour. In order to secure a conviction, Coelius passed his *lex tabellaria*, introducing the method of voting by tablets into the court of *perduellio*, from which it had hitherto been excluded —doluitque, says Cicero (*de Leg*. iii. 16. 36), quoad vixit se ut opprimeret C. Popilium nocuisse rei publicae. The tablet behind the head of Coelius on No. 43 bears the initials of the words *Libero, Damno*. Coelius was praetor in Hispania Citerior about 99,[1] and it is to his achievements in this province that the *vexillum* with the inscription HIS(pania) and the Keltic boar standard refer. The same reference is, according to some authorities, also intended by the shields on the reverse of No. 43 and on the trophies on the reverse of No. 44. The head of the Sun would then perhaps be used in allusion to the names of the family.[2] Still, Borghesi's suggestion that it refers rather to some victory won by a member of the family in the East is tempting. For we find one C. Coelius C.f. (*i.e.*, either the founder of the family or his son) mentioned in the so-called

---

[1] See Wilsdorf in *Leipziger Studien*, i., p. 110.
[2] As Vaillant puts it (*Num. ant. fam. Rom.* i., p. 292; cp. Eckhel, *Num. vet.* v., p. 176): quod sol in coelo videatur et caldus sit.

Senatus consultum Adramyttenum as a Senator of praetorian rank.[1] In the latter case, the circular shield, if not the oblong one, may well represent an Eastern enemy.

The lectisternium type (No. 44)[2] commemorates L. Coelius Caldus, probably a younger son of the elder Caius, and father of the moneyer. He was *septemvir epulonum*, and it is probably he who is represented preparing the *lectum*, on which the gods were supposed to recline at the repast offered to them. A third member of the moneyer's family, probably his uncle, is the C. Caldus mentioned on the same coin as Imp(erator) A(ugur) X(vir sacris faciundis). It is to be noted that the name and titles of this member of the family are written close to the trophies, thus confirming the suggestion that the trophies (and the corresponding shields on the reverse of No. 43) refer not to the Spanish victories of the elder C. Coelius Caldus, but to some exploits of the moneyer's uncle of the same name. These exploits, as we have seen, may have been partly in the East.

---

[1] The date of the inscription is uncertain: Mommsen (*Eph. Epigr.* iv., pp. 216 f.; *Staatsr.* iii., 986 note), supported by Foucart (*Bull. Corr. Hellen.* ix. 401), gives it to 122—120 B.C.; Viereck (*Sermo Graecus*, pp. 22 f.), following Willems, prefers 98—94 B.C., on the ground of its containing this very name, C. Coelius Caldus.

[2] If the curved object attached to the trophy with the oblong shield is a karnyx, and not a *lituus militaris*, then this trophy must refer to a victory over Gauls or Celtiberians. But, even so, the trophy with the round shield may still be Eastern.

HISTORICAL ROMAN COINS

THE CORN LAW OF SATURNINUS.
100 B.C.

45. *Obv.* Head of Saturn r., laureate; behind, a serrated sickle; around, ΠISO.CAEΠIO.Q; below, a trident.

Rev. L. Calpurnius Piso and Q. Servilius Caepio seated on a bench, at each end of which is an ear of corn; in exergue, AD.FRV. EM[V].EX.S.C.

Silver *denarius*. 3·76 grammes (58·0 grains). B.M.C. I., p. 170, No. 1127.

The author of the *Rhetorica ad Herennium* (I. xii. 21) takes as an instance of a legitimate issue arising out of a definition, the question whether Q. Caepio[1] violated the majesty of the Roman people when he prevented the tribune Saturninus from carrying his corn law. He was *quaestor urbanus* at the time, and when L. Appuleius Saturninus proposed his *lex frumentaria de semissibus et trientibus*, by which the state was to let the people buy corn at a *semis* and a *triens* (*i.e.*, ⅚ of an *as*) for a *modius*, he urged that such a dole would break the treasury. The Senate decreed that the measure proposed was unconstitutional. Saturninus defied the veto of his colleagues; Caepio

---

[1] Probably the son of the Q. Caepio who was responsible for the disaster of Arausio in 105, and in whose condemnation Saturninus took a leading part.

thereupon broke up the comitia and for the time
prevented the law being carried; hence the charge
brought against him. It appears from Appian
(*B. C.* i. 30) that Caepio's interference was fruitless,
since the Marian veterans, who swarmed in the city,
in their turn drove Caepio's "viri boni" from the
forum, the voting was resumed, and the Appuleian
law was passed.

Saturninus's proposal reduced the price of corn
per bushel from $6\frac{1}{2}$ *asses* to the nominal sum of $\frac{5}{6}$ *as*.
Numismatic writers have generally assumed that the
lex frumentaria was not carried, but that the Senate
found it necessary to soothe the populace with a dole,
and that they accordingly instructed the quaestors to
buy corn largely, and decreed an appropriation from
the treasury to this end. It would follow that these
coins were struck **EX S**(enatus) **C**(onsulto) **AD FRV**
(mentum) **EMV**(ndum).

As a matter of fact, we know that the Senate (with
the single exception of the stalwart Metellus Numi-
dicus) took the oath to observe the terms of the new
law. The obvious consequence seems to be that they
must have instructed the quaestors to act in accordance
with the law, and procure the necessary corn. The
coins must therefore have been struck in order to
enable the quaestors to carry out the provisions, not of
some *Senatus Consultum* of which we have no other
record, but of the *lex frumentaria* of Saturninus.

HISTORICAL ROMAN COINS

The phrase **EX S.C.** on the coins refers to the order of the Senate for their issue, not to the order for the purchase of corn; *i.e.*, it is to be construed not with *emundum*, but with words meaning "coin struck" understood.[1]

The head of the harvest god Saturn, with the sickle,[2] shown on the obverse, and the ears of corn on the reverse, are obviously appropriate to the occasion. But the primary reason for the use of the obverse type was that the *aerarium populi Romani* which, subject to the sanction of the Senate, provided the urban quaestors with the funds for this expenditure, was situated in the Temple of Saturn below the Capitol.

The trident is a mark to distinguish this particular issue from others, which have an arrow, a bow, etc. Such distinguishing marks do not occur before this date. The substitution for Roma of another deity, on the obverse, is also an innovation.

Caepio's colleague appears to be L. Calpurnius Piso Caesoninus, son of the consul of 112, and father of Cicero's enemy, the consul of 58.

---

[1] Did it refer to the decree for the purchase of the corn, as some suppose (Mommsen-Blacas ii., p. 168), the order of the words should be AD FRV.EX. S.C. EMV.

[2] The form of the sickle is interesting, inasmuch as it corresponds to the toothed form described by Hesiod (*Theog.* 175: καρχαρόδων); whereas ordinarily the attribute of the god resembles the harpa of Perseus. See Daremberg and Saglio, *Dict. Ant.* ii., p. 971.

THE SOCIAL WAR.

90 B.C.

46. *Obv.* Head of Magna Mater r., wearing turreted crown and veil; behind, EX·A·PV.

Rev. Victory in a two-horse chariot r.; before the horses, a bird; under them, C·, and C·FABI· C·F· in exergue.

Silver *denarius*. 4·01 grammes (61·9 grains). B.M.C. I., p. 223, No. 1596.

47. *Obv.* Head of Roma r., helmeted; behind, PV; all in laurel wreath.

Rev. Victory in a two-horse chariot r.; inscr., ML·VCILI·RVF.

Silver *denarius* (edge serrated). 3·95 grammes (61·0 grains). B.M.C. I., p. 224, No. 1613.

It is probable that, in the earlier period of the Roman coinage, all new issues in Rome only took place in accordance with a special decree of the Senate. But after the constitution of the monetary magistracy of the *tresviri aere argento auro flando feriundo*, and even before this had become a regular magistracy, rather than a commission appointed from time to time as necessity demanded, no such special decree of the Senate was needed, the issues being made by the moneyers in virtue of their office. The definitive constitution of the magistracy is placed by Mommsen[1] between 104 and 89 B.C. It is just about

[1] Mommsen-Blacas, ii., pp. 47 f.

this time that formulæ like EX S.C., S.C., ARG(ento) PVB(lico), EX A(rgento) P(ublico), PV(blice), etc., occur most frequently.¹ These phrases indicate special issues which were made in accordance with special decrees either of the Senate or of the people, and not by the *tresviri* in ordinary course. But what exactly is meant by saying that the coins were issued *ex argento publico*? Naturally, the bullion from which all coins were issued by the State must have been public property. We are, it seems, compelled to assume that a reserve of silver in bars² was kept in the public treasury (which continued to be known as the *aerarium populi Romani* long after bronze ceased to be stored there);³ that this reserve was known especially as the *argentum publicum*; and that when in an emergency this reserve had to be converted into coin the source of the metal was indicated in the manner described.

The coins Nos. 46, 47, are dated by external evidence (as of hoards in which they occur) to about 90 B.C., and there can be no doubt that the special circumstances which occasioned the issue of which

---

¹ For more exact dates, see Mommsen-Blacas, ii., pp. 168, 169.

² Pliny (*N. H.* xxxiii. 3. 55) quoting an inventory of the treasury in . . . B.C., gives the amounts of gold and silver, and of silver cash (*numeratum*) separately. He also quotes an inventory of the beginning of the Social War, but the text is injured. It is possible that the occurrence on the coins of the phrase we are discussing, and Pliny's record of an inventory made about the time these coins were struck, are to be connected, and point to some special measures then taken with regard to the treasury (cp. Mommsen-Blacas, ii. p. 407 note).

³ Mommsen-Blacas, ii., p. 72.

they formed part are to be looked for in the Social War. The *denarii* of C. Fabius fall into two groups, both having the same types. In one group, which is without the inscription EX A. PV., the various series are distinguished by Greek letters on the obverse; in the other, which has the inscription just mentioned, the distinguishing letters are Latin, and are placed on the reverse. We may infer that the former group was struck first, and the latter only when it became necessary to encroach on the reserve.

Nothing is known of the moneyers C. Fabius and M. Lucilius Rufus. The bird on the reverse of C. Fabius's *denarii* has been described as a *buteo*, because that word was used as a cognomen by some members of the Fabia gens; but the *buteo* was probably a bird of prey, whereas the creature shown on the coins resembles an ibis or some other long-legged bird. The choice of the Magna Mater for representation on the obverse has probably no historical reason, and we may assume that Fabius selected it on private grounds. The serrated edge seen on the coin of Lucilius [1] is a feature which occurs on Roman silver coins exceptionally in the second century B.C., and commonly from 92 to 70 B.C. The Romans were preceded in this fashion in the years about 200 B.C. by the Carthaginians, by Antiochus III. of Syria, and by Philip V. of Macedon;

---

[1] The notches are not so clearly marked as usual on the specimen illustrated.

the last two use the fashion on bronze coins, the Carthaginians on gold and silver. No explanation of the practice presenting the slightest degree of probability has yet been offered.[1]

THE SOCIAL WAR.
90—81 B.C.

48. *Obv.* Head of Italia r., helmeted; behind, a wreath; below, [✶] **ITALIA**.

Rev. The Dioscuri on horseback; in exergue, in Oscan letters, retrograde, **c · paapi · c ·**

Silver *denarius*. 4·11 grammes (63·5 grains). British Museum.

49. *Obv.* Head of a Bacchante r., wreathed with ivy; in front, in Oscan letters, retrograde, **mutil · embratur.**

Rev. Bull goring wolf; in exergue, in Oscan letters, retrograde, **c · paapi.**

Silver *denarius*. 3·82 grammes (59·0 grains). British Museum.

50. *Obv.* Female head r., laureate; behind, **ITALIA**.

Rev. Young man kneeling, holding a pig, which eight warriors touch with the points of their swords; in the background, a standard upright, in exergue, **Q·SILO**.

Silver *denarius*. Bibliothèque Nationale, Paris.

51. *Obv.* Head of a Bacchante r., wearing ivy wreath.

---
[1] See the various theories in B.M.C., I., p. 159.

HISTORICAL ROMAN COINS

Rev. Cista mystica, with thyrsos, to which a fillet is attached, leaning against it; on the cista, a fawn skin; in the exergue, in Oscan letters, retrograde, **mi · ieiis · mi**.

<small>*Aureus*, 8·47 grammes (130·7 grains). Bibliothèque Nationale, Paris.</small>

52. *Obv.* Helmeted female head (Italia), crowned with wreath by a small figure of Victory from behind.

Rev. Two warriors clasping hands; on the right, prow of a galley, on which are a standard, spears and shields; in exergue, Λ.

<small>Silver *denarius*. Berlin Museum.</small>

These five coins, of which three are unique specimens at Paris or Berlin, are selected from the numerous varieties issued by the Allies during the Social War. The names of both the Marsian Q. Pompaedius Silo and the Samnite C. Papius Mutilus appear. The latter describes himself as "Caius Papius, son of Caius, Mutilus, Imperator." The gold coin is issued by Minius Ieius (Iegius?), son of Minius.

There was no more effective expression of the Allies' defiance of Roman authority than the issue of a coin in gold. The weight of the piece is that of an Attic *stater*. Now just about this time Mithradates, with whom the Allies were in communication, was issuing gold coins on the same standard, in defiance of the Romans, at Pergamum, Athens, and Ephesus.

HISTORICAL ROMAN COINS

The types chosen by the Allies are also significant. Thus Italia—not the country, but the city of Corfinium, which was thus named during the war as destined to be the new capital—is represented, either by a laureate female head, or by a helmeted head copied directly from the Roma on Roman *denarii*. The much-desired defeat of Rome by the Allies is symbolized by the Italic bull goring the Roman wolf.

The alliance with Mithradates is alluded to by the type of two warriors joining hands. One of them wears a diadem, while the prow of a ship—indicating the fleet with which Mithradates was to descend upon Italy—is seen beside them; on the obverse of this coin, the helmeted bust of Italia is crowned by Victory with a wreath.[1]

The scene of the warriors taking an oath over the body of a pig has been explained as an allusion to the treaty of the Caudine Forks. It is more probable that it represents merely the oath taken by the Allies to be faithful to each other against Rome. A similar ceremony (with only two warriors) is shown, as we

[1] Cavedoni and Lenormant (*La Monn. dans l'Antiquité*, ii., pp. 296 f) consider that this piece was struck by the remnant of the revolted Allies to celebrate the disembarkation of Marius on his return from Africa, when the democratic party in Rome had made common cause with the Allies. The type would appear to have been copied by Sulla to celebrate his disembarkation at Brundusium in 83 B.C. after conquering Mithradates; but one would like to be sure of the authenticity of the Sullan coin, which was published in the eighteenth century, and of which no specimen is now known to exist.

have seen, on the earliest Roman gold coinage (No. 11). It is also found on the *denarii* struck by Tiberius Veturius in 92 B.C. There, because T. Veturius Calvinus was one of the two consuls who concluded the treaty of the Caudine Forks, the type has been regarded as alluding to that disgraceful event. If so, it would be unique among the memorial types found on Roman coins; and it is surely singularly perverse to accept such an interpretation when the type may equally well refer to the treaty (also concluded by T. Veturius) giving the Campanians and Samnites the rights of citizenship in 334 B.C. It seems more reasonable, therefore, to regard none of these treaty types as alluding to the Caudine Forks; although, if any of them do so allude, it is the one placed by the Allies on their coins, rather than either of the others.

The significance of the Dionysiac types is obscure. But they may have been partly inspired by the fact that Mithradates posed as the "New Dionysos," the liberator; on his own coins he uses an ivy wreath as a border.

The coins with the names of Papius Mutilus and Pompaedius Silo were probably, as Mommsen points out, struck early in the war; for Mutilus seems to have disappeared from the scene after he was defeated by Sulla in 89 B.C., although he lived some time longer. Silo died in 88 B.C. "The greater number of these coins, and especially those which bear the legend *Italia* or *Viteliu*, must have been struck during the first years of the Social War, when the insurgents still hoped to found a capital which would rival Rome. On the other hand, the rarer coins, bearing the names of Sabine or Samnite chiefs, are of later date, and were struck when Samnium continued to bear alone the burden of the war, and was fighting simply for her own independence."[1]

THE LEX PAPIRIA DE ASSE SEMUNCIALI.
89 B.C.

53. *Obv.* Head of Apollo r., laureate; behind, ⲠISO.
Rev. Riderless horse galloping r.; below, FRVGI; above, E.L.P.

Silver *sestertius*. 0·95 grammes (14·7 grains). B.M.C. I., p. 280, No. 2177.

54. *Obv.* Head of Minerva r., helmeted; [behind, • • • •]
Rev. Prow r.; above, L.P.D.A.P.

Bronze *triens*. 4·41 grammes (68·0 grains). B.M.C. I., p. 282, No. 2192.

By the Lex Papiria (generally but without good reason called the Lex Plautia Papiria), says Pliny,[2] *semunciarii asses facti;* the weight of the *as* was reduced to half an ounce (normally 13·64 grammes or

---

[1] Mommsen-Blacas, ii., p. 424, note.
[2] *N. H.* xxxiii. 3. 46.

210·5 grains). The author of the law was C. Papirius Carbo, tribune of the people in 89 B.C., who, along with M. Plautius Silvanus, carried the famous Lex Plautia Papiria extending the citizenship. This was probably passed quite early in 89 B.C., if not at the close of 90 B.C.;[1] the law with which we are concerned was intimately connected with the policy of extending the franchise, and therefore was also doubtless passed early in the tribunate of Papirius. In a considerable number of cities in Italy, long before the passing of this law, bronze struck on the semuncial standard was in use: e.g., in Calabria, at Brundusium, Orra, and Uxentum; in Lucania, at Copia; in Bruttium, at Vibo Valentia and Petelia. Bronze had by this time already become a mere token coinage. The money of the cities which were now incorporated in the Roman state, and which therefore lost their right of coinage, might have been called in, or tariffed at some arbitrary rate; but what Papirius did was to reduce the legal weight of the Roman *as* to the weight prevailing elsewhere.[2] Very soon afterwards[3] even the Roman mint was closed for bronze, and Italy—once the home of the bronze standard—presents the curious[4]

---

[1] Mommsen, *Rom. Hist.* Vol. iii., p. 247, note.
[2] Mommsen-Blacas, ii., p. 73, note.
[3] About 80 B.C.
[4] Curious, that is to say, at so late a date in history; for previous to the fourth century B.C. little bronze was coined in the ancient world.

spectacle of a country without a bronze coinage, for the few coins which Paestum was for some reason allowed to issue can have made little impression on the currency.

The letters E.L.P. on the *sesterce* No. 53 have been rightly expanded by Borghesi into *E Lege Papiria*; and the letters L.P.D.A.P. explained by Mommsen[1] as *Lege Papiria de aere publico*, by Gaebler[2] as *Lege Papiria de assis pondere*. Of these explanations, Mommsen's is more strongly supported by the analogy of other inscriptions.

The sesterce was issued only twice, the *quinarius* only four times, in the forty years following the Papirian reform, so that the Roman coinage thenceforward consisted of little but *denarii*. L. Calpurnius Piso Frugi himself was responsible, about 88 B.C., for an enormous series of *denarii*, probably the largest ever put out by any one moneyer during the Republic.[3] During the short period 49—44 B.C., small silver was once more issued in some quantities. But how the Romans and Italians can have been content for some 65 years (the bronze coinage was resumed in 15 B.C.) to dispense with the use of bronze, it is puzzling to conceive.

L. Calpurnius Piso Frugi is Cicero's friend. It

---

[1] Mommsen-Blacas, ii., p. 420, note.
[2] *Zeit. f. Num.* 1902, p. 174, note.
[3] The British Museum contains over 270 varieties.

was probably he who, after the end of the Social War, carried the law embodying two new tribes, and who was praetor with Verres in 74 B.C. The Apollo and the horse on his coins refer to the races celebrated at the Ludi Apollinares. These were inaugurated in 212 B.C., and the annual celebration was established next year by Piso's ancestor, C. Calpurnius Piso, praetor urbanus.

SULLA IN GREECE.
87—84 B.C.

55. *Obv.* Head of Venus r.; before it, Cupid standing, holding palm branch; below, L·SVLLA·

Rev. Sacrificial ewer and lituus between two trophies; above and below, IMPER ITERVM·

Aureus. 10·72 grammes (165·4 grains). British Museum.

This *aureus* is one of the earliest specimens of that gold coinage, issued by generals in virtue of their imperium, which eventually developed into the gold coinage of the Empire. Gold issues of this kind were at the time quite outside the province of the ordinary Roman civil moneyer. Apart from that fact, the fabric of the coin proves that it was not produced by the mint at Rome. There is general agreement among numismatists that it should be assigned to the period of Sulla's campaign against Mithradates. During this campaign his quaestor Lucullus issued money in Peloponnesus : Δι' ἐκείνου ἐκόπη τὸ πλεῖστον ἐν Πελοποννήσῳ περὶ τὸν Μιθριδατικὸν πόλεμον, καὶ Λουκούλλειον ἀπ' ἐκείνου προσηγορεύθη, καὶ διετέλεσεν ἐπὶ πλεῖστον, ὑπὸ τῶν στρατιωτικῶν χρειῶν ἐν τῷ πολέμῳ λαμβάνον ἀμοιβὴν ταχεῖαν:[1] the military necessities of the situation caused it to change hands rapidly and to remain long in circulation. Sulla, as is well known, laid all the great temple treasuries of Greece under contribution— Olympia, Delphi, and Epidaurus were plundered— to pay the expenses of his army. Further, after the peace with Mithradates, he levied an indemnity of 20,000 talents on the province of Asia, and this also Lucullus had to convert into coin.[2] It is well known, as we have seen (p. 42), that in such periods of hasty coinage the metal used is more often gold than silver, since gold was the metal which the plundered treasuries afforded more plentifully. Signs of haste are evident in the rude workmanship of these Lucullan coins.

Sulla's idea that he was the favourite of Venus[3] accounts for the representation of her head and of Cupid on his coins. But the palm branch which Cupid holds is the symbol of victory in war. The sacrificial ewer and lituus are indications of priestly office. The two trophies have been explained by

---

[1] Plut. *Lucull.* 2.
[2] *Ibid.* 4. See F. Lenormant, *La Monnaie dans l'Antiquité*, ii., p. 295.
[3] Plut. *Sulla*, 34.

Lenormant as referring to the two salutations as *imperator* received by Sulla—one in Italy, during the Social War, the other in Greece after his first successes there. Von Sallet, however, with much more probability, explains them as trophies of the two victories at Chaeroneia and Orchomenus over Archelaus, the general of Mithradates, in 86 and 85 B.C.[1] The *aureus* must therefore date from the year 85 at the earliest.

The weight of Sulla's first *aureus* is about $\frac{1}{30}$ of the Roman pound (its normal weight should be 10·915 grammes). Later *aurei* were struck at $\frac{1}{36}$ (Sulla and Pompeius), $\frac{1}{38}$ (Caesar), and $\frac{1}{42}$ (Augustus), and so on in regular decrease to the time of Constantine.

POMPEIUS IN AFRICA.

81 B.C.

56. *Obv*. Head of Africa in elephant-skin head-dress between ewer and lituus; behind, **MAGNVS**; all in wreath.

Rev. A triumphal quadriga containing a person holding a palm branch and crowned by a flying Victory; on one of the horses, a boy holding a palm branch and wand; in exergue, **PRO·COS**.

Aureus. 8·93 grammes (137·8 grains). British Museum.

Zeit. f. Num. xii., p. 381. These same trophies occur on a contemporary tetradrachm with Athenian types evidently struck by Sulla in Greece (B.M.C. *Attica*, p. lv).

HISTORICAL ROMAN COINS

Pompeius, having in 82 B.C. as propraetor recovered Sicily, proceeded in the next year to Africa, in order to deal with Domitius Ahenobarbus and Hiarbas, the usurper of the Numidian throne. His victory was easy. The events which followed are well known: the attempt of the Senate to disband his army, and to baulk him of his triumph, which, as a matter of fact, being an extraordinary magistrate, he could not constitutionally claim; his protest, and Sulla's concession. When Pompeius returned to Rome, Sulla greeted him as "Magnus." That title had already been given him by his troops in Africa,[1] and Sulla was wise enough to defer to their opinion. So Pompeius, who was only 24 years old, and not yet even a senator, triumphed: eques Romanus, id quod antea nemo, curru triumphali revectus.[2]

This *aureus* undoubtedly refers to a triumph, which the head of Africa on the obverse identifies, with a strong degree of probability, as the triumph after the African victories.[3] But where and when was the coin struck? Not in Rome, for gold coins like this were issued by military commanders, in virtue of their

---

[1] See Plutarch, *Pomp.* 13.
[2] Plin. *N.H.* vii. 96; Liv. *Ep.* lxxxix. Cp. Licinian. Gran. p. 39: et Pompeius annos natus xxv. eques Romanus, quod nemo antea, propraetore ex Africa triumphavit iiii. idus Martias.
[3] So Mommsen-Blacas, ii., p. 456, note. But it is straining a point to argue that the head of Africa also alludes to Pompeius' grand elephant hunt or to his idea of triumphing in a car drawn by elephants.

imperium, and only outside the city. Probably in Spain, whither Pompeius proceeded in 77 B.C. as proconsul. This accords with the inscription on the coin. Mommsen, it is true, associating the inscription directly with the African triumph, has some difficulty in explaining the title PROCOS. He notes that (according to Licinianus) Pompeius, on his return from Africa, triumphed with the title *pro praetore*; but he explains that between this title and that of *pro consule* there is a distinction only of rank, not of authority. Pompeius, having been despatched to Sicily and Africa with an extraordinary imperium, without holding or having held any magistracy, might well have assumed the title *pro consule* in Africa, and triumphed as *pro praetore* in Rome! "Tout le reste s'explique facilement." The extreme subtlety of such an explanation becomes entirely unnecessary if we suppose that the coin was issued when Pompeius was actually proconsul, but before the glory of his African triumph had been dimmed by greater exploits. That was the case when he was fighting Sertorius in Spain from 76 to 72 B.C. The circumstances of the campaign might very naturally demand the issue of a military coinage in gold such as we have before us.

Other dates which have been suggested for the coin are 71 B.C. (the Spanish triumph) and 61 B.C. (the Asian triumph). In considering these alternatives we have always to remember that the gold coins must have been issued in some province, not in Rome. Therefore they cannot have been produced actually on the occasion of the triumph to which they refer;[1] since in order to triumph Pompeius had to be in Rome. It follows that, if they allude to the Spanish triumph, they cannot have been struck until he next went out with military imperium—viz., in 67 B.C., to the East; if to the Asian triumph, it would seem, on similar grounds, that they must date from his proconsulship in Spain, which began in 55 B.C.

The fabric of the coins gives us little assistance; it does not seem to be indisputably Eastern, and of the fabric of coins struck in Spain we know too little to speak decisively.

One other point has to be considered. If the boy who rides on one of the horses is the son of Pompeius, the younger Cneius, then the triumph cannot be the African one, since Cneius was still unborn at the time. But, as Mommsen points out, the honour of so riding was often given to relatives when sons were

---

[1] It has indeed been suggested, at least in connexion with certain analogous "triumphal" pieces of Sulla, that they were struck shortly before the triumph to serve for largess. But there is no foundation for such a statement, and it is significant that the Sullan pieces in question are rarely found in Italy, and were evidently issued and circulated chiefly in the East. The coin of Pompeius before us is extremely rare, only two or three specimens being known.

HISTORICAL ROMAN COINS

not available.[1] This argument, therefore, carries no weight.

We are thus, it would appear, free to choose among the various available dates, and the period of the first Spanish proconsulship seems to have more in its favour than the rest; since, other things being equal, we are then able to connect both obverse and reverse with the same event, and that an event of fairly recent date.

The weight of the coin shows that it was struck on the standard of 36 to the Roman pound.

THE SUBJECTION OF KING ARETAS.

62 B.C.

57. *Obv.* King Aretas kneeling r. beside a camel, holding an olive-branch; above, M. SCAVR.AED.CVR·; below, EX S.C. REX ARETAS.

Rev. Jupiter in a quadriga l., hurling a thunderbolt; below horses' feet, a scorpion; above, Γ· HVΓSAEVS AED·CVR·; below, C. HVΓSAE COS.ΓREIVER.CAΓTV.

Silver *denarius*. 3·76 grammes (58·0 grains). B.M.C. I., p. 484, No. 3878.

Aretas III., king of the Nabathaeans, interfered more than once in the affairs of Syria and Judaea.

---

[1] Mommsen suggests that in this case it is Sextus Pompeius (first cousin once removed of the triumvir), who was born about 95 B.C.

He ruled for a time in Damascus; defeated the Jewish king Alexander Jannaeus at Addida, and besieged king Aristobulus in Jerusalem (65 B.C.). M. Aemilius M. f. M. n. Scaurus, sent against him by Pompeius, frightened him away; but although during his retreat he was defeated by Aristobulus, he was far from crushed, and continued to give trouble. Pompeius, unable to take the field himself, sent Scaurus once more, and in 62 B.C. Aretas made peace, obtaining good terms. That did not prevent Scaurus from representing the king as a suppliant, who has dismounted from his camel and kneels, proffering an olive-branch. This is the earliest instance of a Roman moneyer commemorating on his coins his own exploits.

The piece before us belongs to an issue made specially (*ex Senatus consulto*) on the occasion of the aedilician games celebrated by Scaurus in 58 B.C. These games were notorious for their insane extravagance: 150 panthers, five crocodiles, the bones (forty feet long) of the very monster to which Andromeda was said to have been exposed at Joppa in Judaea, were amongst the attractions which he provided[1] and which helped to ruin his fortunes and the morality of the populace.[2] His colleague in the aedileship was P. Plautius Hypsaeus, who had also been in the

---

[1] Pliny *N. H.* viii. 64; 96; ix. 11.
[2] Pliny *N. H.* xxxvi. 113.

service of Pompeius as quaestor. The scorpion may indeed refer to some exploit performed by Hypsaeus in the province of Commagene, of which it is the emblem.[1] The significance of the type of Jupiter fulminating is obscure; for the suggestion that the god is meant, as Ζεὺς ὕψιστος, to refer to the name of the moneyer, is not very attractive. After all, the type was an old one. But the legend appears to connect it definitely in some way with the capture of Privernum by the moneyer's ancestor, the consul C. Plautius.[2] This feat marked the final subjection of the Volscians in 329 B.C.[3] Probably[4] the type refers to the consul's triumph after his Volscian campaign; for it must be remembered that in a triumph the victorious general appeared in the character and guise of Jupiter.

The form CAPTV (for *captum*) is less probably an instance of *anousvara*—i.e., the suppression of M in writing—than an abbreviation caused by lack of space.

CAESAR IN ROME.
49 B.C.

58. *Obv.* Female head r., wearing wreath of oak-leaves, and jewellery; behind ⊥II.

---

[1] But it occurs only on one of the two (or three) series of coins struck by Hypsaeus, so that it is more probably a differentiating mark of some kind.

[2] His cognomen seems to have been Decianus, not Hypsaeus as the coin gives it.

[3] Liv. viii. 20.

[4] As Mommsen (ii., p. 491 note) seems to imply.

HISTORICAL ROMAN COINS

Rev. Trophy of Gaulish arms (tunic, horned helmet, shield and karnyx); on r., an axe adorned with an animal's head; across field, **CAE SAR**.

Aureus. 8·50 grammes (131·2 grains). B.M.C. I., p. 505, No. 3954.

59. *Obv.* Similar to preceding.

Rev. Similar trophy; at its foot, figure of a prisoner, seated, with hands tied behind him; across field, **CAE SAR**.

Silver *denarius.* 3·37 grammes (52 grains). B.M.C. I., p. 506, No. 3959.

60. *Obv.* Head of Apollo, r., hair confined by fillet; below, star; around, **Q·SICINIVS III·VIR**.

Rev. Club and lion-skin between bow and arrow; around, **C·COPON[IVS] ·PR·S·C·**

Silver *denarius.* 3·99 grammes (61·6 grains). British Museum.

When Caesar entered Rome in 49, he naturally seized the state treasure in the temple of Saturn, and converted it into coin for the payment of his troops. The gold and silver coins, Nos. 58 and 59, form part of this issue, which is remarkable in many ways. Roman commanders had previously issued a military coinage distinct from the regular urban coinage; thus Lucullus, acting as quaestor for Sulla in the Mithradatic war, had struck gold pieces in his commander's name (see No. 55). But here we have the general striking a military coinage in Rome itself, while the only approach to a regular urban coinage was being struck outside Rome! Thus there are *denarii* (No. 60) issued in this year for the praetor C. Coponius, who was in command of the fleet at Rhodes, by the monetary triumvir Q. Sicinius. Constitutionally Q. Sicinius, as home magistrate, had no right to issue a military coinage; he placed himself within his rights by adding the letters S.C. The inverted position of affairs, caused by Caesar's occupation of the capital, could not be better illustrated. But Caesar's coinage, irregular as it seems, was none the less the foundation of the imperial gold coinage, which is, strictly speaking, an imperatorial coinage issued from the Roman mint.

The goddess represented on the obverse of Caesar's coins is generally identified with Pietas, because this name is inscribed against a somewhat similar head on a contemporary coin of Decimus Brutus. But the head on Brutus's coin has no oak-wreath, an attribute which must surely be significant. The amount of jewellery which the goddess wears (earring, necklace, and pearls—apparently—on the knot in which her hair is tied behind) suggests that Eckhel[1] was right in calling her Venus, who would obviously be appropriate as the divine ancestress of the Julian family. But there appears to be no evidence that

---

[1] *Doctrina Num. Vet.* vi. p. 6.

HISTORICAL ROMAN COINS

Venus was ever represented with the oak-wreath. The identification must, therefore, for the present be regarded as uncertain.

The numerals LII (52)[1] have been explained as an indication of Caesar's age. This is not so absurd as it may at first sight seem. The legates of M. Antonius, on coins struck in Gaul in 42 and 41 B.C., indicated the triumvir's age (see Nos. 76, 77). Caesar was probably born in 102 B.C., not in 100, as is generally supposed.[2] Thus in the year 49 he would have completed his fifty-second year. The reason for stating his age would be to remind the Romans that in the next year he would constitutionally be entitled to hold the consulship for the second time. (If the coins were distributed on Caesar's birthday the mention of his age would have additional significance.) No man, by the *lex annalis*, could hold the consulship before he had entered on his forty-third year. An interval of eleven years was required between two consulships. Caesar, now in his fifty-third year, would in 48 B.C. be once more eligible. The trophy, on the other hand, served to recall Caesar's exploits in Gaul, the shaggy-headed prisoner represented on the reverse of the *denarius* being probably no other than Vercingetorix.[3]

---

[1] For so they must be interpreted, rather than as the letters IIT.
[2] See the note in Mommsen's *History of Rome*, bk. v., chap. i.
[3] See Babelon, *Rev. Num.* 1902, pp. 1 ff. On coins of Hostilius Saserna, struck about 48 B.C., we have the heads of Vercingetorix and of the oak-wreathed goddess described above.

The shield, helmet, and war-trumpet are typically Gaulish; but it may be doubted whether the axe is not a form of sacrificial axe rather than a barbarian weapon. An axe decorated with a lion's head is represented among the sacrificial implements on *denarii* of P. Sulpicius Galba issued about 69 B.C.;[1] and an actual bronze axe with a bull's head was in the Forman Collection.[2] In the present case, a wolf's head seems to have been employed as ornament.

These *aurei* and *denarii* of Caesar are alike extremely rare. The *aurei* were struck at 38 to the Roman pound of 327·45 grammes, evidently with the object of approximating as closely as possible to one of the many forms of the "gold-shekel" standard which had been almost universal in the Eastern Mediterranean from time immemorial. Soon afterwards the standard was lowered to 40 to the pound, or 8·18 grammes. As the gold coins continued to be worth the same number of *denarii* (25), the older, heavier ones were probably melted down. This would account for their rarity, but hardly for the rarity of the *denarii*.

THE SENATORIAL PARTY IN THE PROVINCES.
49 B.C.

61. *Obv.* Young male head r., hair confined with fillet; around, L LENT.C.MARC.COS (NT and MA ligatured).

[1] Grueber, B. M. C. i., p. 433, Nos. 3516 f.
[2] C. Smith, *Catal. of the Forman Collection*, No. 160.

Rev. Jupiter standing, holding eagle and thunderbolt; at his feet, altar; in field l., star and Q.

Silver *denarius*. 3·75 grammes (57·8 grains). British Museum.

62. *Obv.* Winged Gorgon's head in the middle of the three-legged symbol (triskeles) of Sicily; between the legs, ears of barley.

Rev. Jupiter standing, holding eagle and thunderbolt; in field r., pruning-hook; on r. and l.: **LENT.MAR.COS** (**NT** and **MAR** ligatured).

Silver *denarius*. 4·12 grammes (63·6 grains). British Museum.

L. Lentulus Crus and C. Claudius Marcellus were chosen consuls for the year 49 B.C. Both, more especially Lentulus, were declared enemies of Caesar, and fled hastily at his approach to Rome. Early in March they were sent forward by Pompeius to Epirus. During the time of Caesar's Spanish expedition, Lentulus seems to have been occupied in raising troops in the East, but he returned in time for the fighting in Epirus. Of Marcellus we hardly hear again; in 48 B.C. he was, with Coponius, in command of the Rhodian squadron.

Of the two coins bearing the names of the consuls, the first was issued by a quaestor (hence the letter Q on the reverse), either at the Pompeian headquarters, Dyrrhachium, or else at Apollonia. The latter mint is perhaps the more probable, since in the obverse type we may recognize Apollo, whose head is the regular type of the silver "*denarii*" of Apollonia in the first century B.C. The second coin, on the other hand, bears a symbol which definitely connects it with Sicily. For, whatever may have been the original meaning of the triskeles,[1] there is no doubt that, at the time when these coins were struck, it recalled the three-cornered island of Sicily to the Romans as clearly as the same symbol recalls to us the Isle of Man. Now of any actual visit of the consuls to Sicily in their year of office we have no record; and as our information with regard to their movements, from the time of their leaving Rome to their departure from Brundisium, is fairly detailed, we may well doubt whether they went to Sicily at all. But Pompeius was actively employed, until he left Italy, in raising men and money from every source.[2] It is improbable that he would have neglected Sicily, especially as it was held for the Senate by Marcus Cato, until the approach of Curio drove him to join Pompeius. We may therefore not unreasonably conjecture that these coins were struck in the name of the consuls, in connexion with the levies of men, provisions, or money, which were being made on the island by the Senatorial party. The ears of barley

[1] On this see an interesting note by J. Six in *Sertum Nabericum* (1908), where it is suggested that the triskeles is the symbol of thunder.

[2] Cass. Dio. xli. 9.7.

HISTORICAL ROMAN COINS

attached to the triskeles remind us that Sicily was one of the great sources of corn-supply.

The figure of Jupiter is common to the two issues. It is of course possible that in the one case it has some local reference, while in the other it is merely retained without any particular significance. Thus, if the Sicilian issue is the earlier, as is probable, the figure may represent some statue of Zeus in Sicily. Furtwängler,[1] accordingly, approves Havercamp's conjecture that it is meant for the Syracusan Zeus Eleutherios. Further, he maintains that these coins need not have been struck in or for Sicily at all, but that the Sicilian types are personal to the consul Marcellus, who was descended from the conqueror of the island. It seems however improbable that the types of both sides of the coin with the triskeles should refer to Marcellus, leaving Lentulus in the cold. A satisfactory explanation of the Jupiter type has still to be discovered.

CAESAR'S FOURFOLD TRIUMPH.

46 B.C.

63. *Obv.* Veiled beardless head r.; around, **C.CAESAR COS.TER**.

Rev. Lituus, ewer and axe; below, **A·HIRTIVS PR**.

Aureus. 8·07 grammes (124·6 grains). B.M.C. I., p. 525, No. 4050.

[1] *Masterpieces*, p. 218.

HISTORICAL ROMAN COINS

The third consulship of Julius Caesar dates this coin to the year 46 B.C. It was struck by Caesar's lieutenant A. Hirtius,[1] the continuator of the "Gallic War," who abbreviates the name of his magistracy thus: PR. Does this mean *Praetor*, or *Praefectus urbi?* The former is the more probable, since there is no certain instance of the abbreviation PR standing *alone*, without the qualifying dative or genitive VRB(i) or VRB(is), being used on a coin for *praefectus*. When, as in the coins of C. Clovius, the qualifying word is omitted, the abbreviation is PRAEF.[2] Historically, the choice before us is an even one; for we know that in or for the year with which we are concerned Caesar arranged for the appointment of six *praefecti* of the city and ten praetors.[3] Hirtius may have been either, and as either may have issued the coin in question. On the whole, the evidence, from a linguistic standpoint, favours the interpretation of the abbreviation as *Praetor*.

An examination of a number of these coins shows that they are hastily and carelessly struck from, as a

---

[1] On Hirtius, see Max L. Strack in *Bonner Jahrbücher*, Heft 118.

[2] Whether Clovius is meant to be described as *praefectus urbis* or *praefectus classis* (or even *praefectus fabrum*, as Münzer suggests, in Pauly-Wissowa *s.n.*) does not affect the argument. The coins of Q. Oppius call him PR, but there is nothing to prove that this means *praefectus*. Cestius and Norbanus, also called PR, were most probably praetors.

[3] Cassius Dio, xlii. 51 and xliii. 28.

HISTORICAL ROMAN COINS

rule, rather roughly executed dies. There can be little doubt that this coinage—which, it must be remembered, was not the ordinary silver coinage of the triumvirs of the mint, but a special issue of gold—was intended to serve for the enormous largesses which Caesar squandered at his triumphs in 46 B.C. He gave, for instance, to each veteran foot-soldier, 20,000 *sesterces*, *i.e.* 200 such *aurei*; to each of the populace, in addition to a dole of corn and oil, 400 *sesterces*, *i.e.* 4 such *aurei*.[1] The enormous coinage which must have been required explains the rudeness with which the coins are executed, and their comparative plentifulness at the present time. The types do not seem to carry any allusion to the events of the year. The head on the obverse is generally described as Pietas—a name which is somewhat indiscriminately applied by numismatists to any veiled head of somewhat feminine appearance. When we remember how common a religious rite was the veiling of the head, the doubtfulness of such an identification is apparent. Nevertheless here, where the type of the reverse alludes to Caesar's position as religious head of the state, it is quite reasonable to suppose that the obverse represents Pietas, or the sense of duty towards the gods, the outward sign of which, as we know from Lucretius's protest,[2] was the veiling

[1] Suetonius, *Divus Iulius*, 38.
[2] Bk. V. 1198.

HISTORICAL ROMAN COINS

of the head before the sacred images of the gods :—

> nec pietas ullast, velatum saepe videri
> vertier ad lapidem atque omnis accedere ad aras.

CORINTH REFOUNDED.

44 B.C.

64. *Obv.* Head of Julius Caesar r., laureate; behind, **LAVS·IVLI·CORINT (INT** ligatured).

Rev. Bellerophon mounted on Pegasus r., striking downwards with spear; above and below, **[L·CERTO·AEFICIO C]·IVLIO·IIVIR (AE** ligatured).

Bronze. 5·27 grammes (81·4 grains). B.M.C. *Corinth*, p. 58, No. 487.

65. *Obv.* Bellerophon, wearing petasos and chlamys, walking r., leading Pegasus by the bridle, before an arched doorway. In exergue, **CORINTHVM·**

Rev. Poseidon seated r. on rock, r. hand resting on knee, l. holding long trident upright; on r. **[P·]TADI·CHILO**, on l. **C·IVLI· NICEP·II·VIR.**

Bronze. 8·34 grammes (128·7 grains). B.M.C. *Corinth*, p. 58, No. 484.

The recolonization of Corinth and Carthage was intended by Julius Caesar at the same time as an "atonement for two of the worst crimes committed by the old Republic, and as a means not only of relieving the capital of the world of starving proletarians, but also of vigorously enforcing the Romanization of the subject provinces."[1] Corinth began to rise from its ruins probably one hundred and two years after Mummius sacked it—*i.e.*, in 44 B.C.; whether actually before the murder of the dictator or not, it is difficult to say. For the fact that the foundation is definitely ascribed by many ancient writers to Caesar merely means that he made the necessary plans before his death. It has indeed been maintained that the real foundation was only effected by the triumvirs after the battle of Philippi. The numismatic evidence, on the whole, favours an earlier date.[2] For the duoviri L. Certus Aeficius and C. Iulius, who strike coins with the head of Julius Caesar, do not represent the heads of M. Antonius or Octavian, as they might be expected to do if their term of office had fallen after the campaign of Philippi. Further, the full title of the colony, Laus Iuli(a) Corint(hus), which, on the coins certainly of the time of Antonius, Augustus and the earlier emperors down to Domitian, is replaced by the form **CORINT** or **CORINTHI**, would be expected on the earliest coins.

---

[1] Hertzberg, *Gesch. Griechenlands*, i., pp. 460 f.; where also the varying views as to the date of the foundation are discussed.
[2] On the chronology of the coins, see Earle Fox, in *Journal International d'Archéologie Numismatique*, ii. (1899), pp. 94 f.

HISTORICAL ROMAN COINS

The coin of the duoviri P. Tadius Chilo and C. Iulius Niceporus, which is also for various reasons placed early in the series, bears the legend *Corinthum*. This use of the accusative is not paralleled elsewhere, and is difficult to explain.

The types are local. The standing type of the coinage of Corinth from the earliest times was Pegasus. Bellerophon himself was less commonly represented. On one of our coins he is seen leading Pegasus—having evidently but just tamed him—towards the doorway of a building of some kind; possibly this is meant to indicate the fountain-house of Peirene. On the other, we have part of the battle with the Chimaera—without the Chimaera. It is not certain whether the figure of Poseidon reproduces an actual statue.[1]

The coins are signed by the *duoviri iure dicundo*, the highest officials of the colony, as eponymous magistrates.

THE MURDER OF CAESAR.

44 B.C.

66. *Obv.* Head of Julius Caesar r., laureate, veiled; in front, **CAESAR**; behind, **DICT. PERPETVO**.

---

[1] See Imhoof-Blumer and Gardner, *Numism. Comm. on Pausanias*, pp. 16 f., for the various Poseidon statues at Corinth.

HISTORICAL ROMAN COINS

Rev. Venus standing to l. with sceptre (at foot of which is a shield) in her l., and a Victory in her r.; on r., P·SEPVLLIVS; on l., MACER.

Silver *denarius*. 3·85 grammes (59·4 grains). B.M.C. I., p. 549, No. 4173.

67. *Obv.* Head of M. Antonius r., bearded, veiled; in front, lituus; behind, one-handled jug. Circular countermark.

Rev. Horseman riding at a gallop and leading a second horse to r.; behind, wreath and palm-branch; above, P·SEPVLLIVS; below, MACER.

Silver *denarius*. 4·28 grammes (66·0 grains). B.M.C. I., p. 550, No. 4178.

The exact date of these coins has been much discussed, though the choice of years lies only between 44 and 43 B.C. The second piece, showing the head of M. Antonius with the beard which he grew in sign of mourning, must obviously have been struck after the death of Caesar, March 15th, 44 B.C. The first, on which Caesar is called "Dictator perpetuo," must accordingly date after the beginning of 44 B.C. Another *denarius* of Macer represents the temple which the Senate proposed, shortly before the Dictator's death, to erect to his clemency;[1] Clementia and Caesar were represented joining hands, and this virtue

---

[1] Plut. *Caes.* 57; App. *b.c.* ii. 106; Cass. Dio, xliv. 6.

thus entered the ranks of the gods publicly worshipped at Rome. Although the temple is represented on the coin of Macer, it by no means follows that it was actually completed at the time.[1]

There is thus no cogent reason for postponing the magistracy of Macer until 43 B.C.; indeed, since Antonius left Rome at the end of November, 44, and was thenceforward active against the Senate, being in fact declared a public enemy after his defeat by Hirtius in April, 43, it is difficult to see how the Senate could have allowed a moneyer of the latter year to place the head of Antonius on the coins.[2] So far, Caesar's was the only portrait of a living person that had appeared on the Roman coinage, and that in accordance with a special decree of the Senate.[3] The privilege would not have been repeated for Antonius during the period of strained relations with the Senate; or for him alone, without Lepidus and Octavian, during the triumvirate. Again, when the triumvirate came into being, late in the year, Caesar had been dead for

[1] Any more than the Tempio Malatestiano at Rimini was completed in the form represented on Matteo de' Pasti's medal of Sigismondo Malatesta, which was cast in 1450 to show the elevation planned by the architect Leone Battista Alberti.

[2] See Grueber, B.M.C. i., p. 548.

[3] Cassius Dio, xliv. 4. What Dio says is: Πατέρα τε αὐτὸν τῆς πατρίδος ἐπωνόμοσαν καὶ ἐς τὰ νομίσματα ἐνεχάραξαν. A better writer would have inserted a word making it clear that it was Caesar's portrait, and not his title *Pater Patriae*, which was engraved on the coins; but there can be no doubt as to the real significance of the passage.

more than eighteen months, and the Caesarian types would have lost much of their point. We may therefore accept De Salis's attribution of these coins to the year of Caesar's death. The first was probably struck before the fatal event. Caesar is represented with veiled head as *pontifex maximus*. The portrait, though not nearly so well executed as the head on the coins of L. Aemilius Buca, another moneyer of the same year, is more like the traditional Caesar. He wears the laurel-wreath, the perpetual use of which was granted to him by the State, much, says Suetonius,[1] to his satisfaction, because his baldness exposed him to the derision of his enemies. Venus is represented on the coin as the ancestress of the Julian house; she is here the Venus Victrix whose name was Caesar's watchword at Pharsalus and Munda,[2] and whom he had represented on his signet-ring.[3] On the second coin the palm-branch and wreath show that the type is agonistic; the rider is a *desultor*, and the contest that in which a horseman leaps from one horse to another in full gallop. Suetonius records[4] that *nobilissimi iuvenes* rode in such races at the Circensian games celebrated by Caesar. As this performance by young men of good position was something out of the common, Macer may have thought it a suitable type for coins

---

[1] *Divus Iulius*, 45.
[2] Appian *b.c.* ii. 68. 281; 104. 430.
[3] Cassius Dio, xliii. 43.
[4] *Divus Iulius* 39.

HISTORICAL ROMAN COINS

so closely connected with Caesar or his memory. The same type is used as the reverse of the coins with the temple of Clementia.

BRUTUS IN ASIA AND MACEDON.
43—42 B.C.

68. *Obv.* Head of Brutus r.; on l. **BRVTVS**, on r. **IMP**; the whole in a wreath.

Rev. Military and naval trophy; on l. **CASCA**, on r. **LONGVS**.

<small>*Aureus.* 8·64 grammes (133·3 grains). British Museum.</small>

69. *Obv.* Head of Brutus r.; behind, **L·PLAET·CEST**; above and in front, **BRVT IMP**.

Rev. Cap of Liberty between two daggers; **EID·MAR**.

<small>Silver *denarius.* 3·80 grammes (58·7 grains). British Museum.</small>

70. *Obv.* Bust of Liberty r., veiled; around, **L·SESTI· PROQ·**

Rev. Tripod, axe, and sacrificial ladle; around, **Q·CAEPIO BRVTVS PROCOS·**

<small>Silver *denarius.* 3·84 grammes (59·3 grains). British Museum.</small>

71. *Obv.* Head of Brutus r.

Rev. Four-legged seat (*subsellium*) between viator's wand (*virga*) and money-chest (*fiscus*); below, **Q**.

<small>Bronze. 9·36 grammes (144·5 grains). British Museum.</small>

Of these coins, No. 68 was struck in Asia Minor, during the year 43, when Brutus was preparing for the campaign of Philippi; the others in 42, when he was in Macedon. The name of Brutus, as the adopted son of Q. Servilius Caepio, has on No. 70 the official form Q. Caepio Brutus. Besides him, the coins name three of his officers. L. Plaetorius Cestianus is unknown to history. L. Sestius, who strikes as *pro quaestore*, is that attractive person, the devoted friend of Brutus, to whom Horace addressed an ode (I.4), and whom Augustus took into his favour. Casca Longus is Servilius Casca: either Publius, who was the first to strike at Caesar,[1] or his brother Caius.[2] Publius served as the legatus of Brutus, fought at Philippi, and died soon afterwards. Caius, who was also among the conspirators, was, like his brother, present in the campaign of Philippi. The bronze piece, No. 71, does not, strictly speaking, come into the ordinary Roman series. From comparison with other coins it is clear that it was struck in Macedon, and probably at Pella or Thessalonica, shortly before the campaign of Philippi.[3]

The types for the most part explain themselves. The cap of liberty between the two daggers, with the inscription commemorating the Ides of March, has an extraordinarily modern flavour. The sacrificial instruments on No. 70 must refer to some priestly office.

[1] Cic. *Phil.* ii. 11; Plut. *Caes.* 66; *Brut.* 17, 45; Cass. Dio, xliv. 52; xlvi. 49.

[2] Cic. *ibid.*; App. ii. 113; Cass. Dio, xliv. 52.

[3] Imhoof-Blumer, *Monnaies grecques*, p. 60, No. 1.

HISTORICAL ROMAN COINS

The trophy on Casca's coin commemorates the petty victories which the tyrannicides won over the unfortunate Asiatics in the year before Philippi. On the reverse of the bronze coin we find the insignia of the quaestor who issued it (marking it accordingly with the letter **Q**).

THE TRIUMVIRS.
Nov. 43—Dec. 38 b.c.

72. *Obv.* Head of M. Antonius r.; around, **M·ANTONIVS·III·VIR·R·P·C·**

   Rev. Heroic figure (Anton) seated l. on rocks, with spear and shield; around, **L· REGVLVS·IIII·VIR·A·P·F.**

   Aureus. 7·98 grammes (123·1 grains). B.M.C. I., p. 578, No. 4255.

73. *Obv.* Head of Octavian r.; around, **C·CAESAR III·VIR·R·P·C.**

   Rev. Aeneas carrying Anchises r.; around, inscription as on preceding.

   Aureus. 8·24 grammes (127·1 grains). B.M.C. I., p. 579, No. 4258.

74. *Obv.* Head of Lepidus r.; around, **M·LEPIDVS· III·VIR·R·P·C.**

   Rev. The Vestal Aemilia standing l., holding simpulum and sceptre; around, inscription as on No. 72.

   Aureus. 7·98 grammes (123·2 grains). B.M.C. I., p. 580, No. 4259.

HISTORICAL ROMAN COINS

L. Livineius Regulus issued these coins as one of the *quattuorviri auro publico feriundo*. Other moneyers who struck gold coins with the same title about the same time are L. Mussidius Longus and P. Clodius M. f. All three men issued sets of three gold coins with portraits of the triumvirs; and C. Vibius Varus, though he does not describe himself as belonging to the quattuorvirate, has an analogous issue. It seems natural, therefore, to assign these four moneyers to the same year, viz., the first year of the triumvirate, 43—42 B.C. De Salis, however, on various numismatic grounds with which we need not concern ourselves here, gives the coins of Mussidius and Regulus to the year 39, and postpones the issues of the two others to the next year. It was in 44 B.C. that Caesar raised the number of moneyers from three to four. De Salis's view was that only two of the board of four exercised their right of coinage in each year. And he supposed the portraits of the triumvirs to have appeared, not in the first year of the triumvirate, but after the third partition of the Empire at the treaty of Brundisium.

However this may be—and De Salis's position has been shaken in some details by the discovery of coins unknown to him—the historical interest of these issues does not depend entirely on their exact date. We have already noticed the gradual intrusion of the gold imperatorial coinage into the system of the Roman mint. The process is now complete; these gold coins are part of the regular currency, struck by the regularly appointed officials of the mint, without reference to the military imperium. Equally important, however, is the emphasis laid on the personalities of the triumvirs. The portrait of Julius Caesar was the first to appear, quite irregularly, as the portrait of a living person, on the coins;[1] then, in exceptional circumstances, came the portrait of M. Antonius; now, with the portraits of the *triumviri reipublicae constituendae* side by side before us, we no longer feel that there is anything exceptional in the portrayal of the living rulers of the state. Another blow has been struck at the "republican" nature of the coinage. On the coins of Q. Voconius Vitulus and Ti. Sempronius Gracchus, which De Salis has attributed to 37 B.C., the heads of Antonius and Lepidus do not occur, and their absence illustrates the growing power of Octavian, who alone, with Divus Julius, is represented. This is the next stage. Finally, after this year, not even the names of the quattuorviri or other moneyers are inscribed on the coins, while the types refer wholly to Octavian, not to the moneyer's family history; we have, to all intents and purposes, reached the full imperial stage of the coinage. With the revival of the bronze or brass coinage in 16 B.C., the moneyers' names reappeared

---

[1] On the significance of the portraits of living persons on Roman coins, see Macdonald, *Coin Types*, pp. 192 f.

HISTORICAL ROMAN COINS

for a brief period, and the Senate's authority was recognized, in that this money bore the letters **S C** (*Senatus consulto*). These letters, indeed, continued to mark, with few exceptions, all the coins of copper, bronze or brass, for nearly two and a-half centuries, as issued by the authority of the Senate. But the gold and silver coinage always retained the character which had been given it in the years with which we are dealing. The imperial coinage of Rome thus begins not with the year 27 B.C., but some ten years earlier.

The types on the reverses here described are obvious in their personal reference. Anton, son of Hercules, was claimed by the Antonii as the founder of their race. Aeneas appears on the coins of Octavian as founder of the Iulii. The Vestal is presumably the Aemilia who, when the fire of which she was in charge went out, prayed to the goddess and, throwing a piece of her robe on the embers, miraculously rekindled the flame. Yet the Romans who saw a Vestal represented on the coins of an Aemilius could hardly fail to remember first of all the scandal of the Vestal Aemilia who for her unchastity paid the penalty of death in 114 B.C.

CASSIUS AT RHODES.
43 B.C.

75. *Obv.* Head of Liberty r., laureate; behind, C·CASSEI·IMP.

Rev. Crab holding in its claws an *aplustre*; below, a diadem and a half-blown rose; on l. M·SERVILIVS, on r. LEG.

Silver *denarius*. 3·84 grammes (59·2 grains). British Museum.

Cassius, having crushed Dolabella in Syria, returned to meet Brutus in Asia. Before proceeding to Macedonia he undertook to punish the adherents of the triumvirs in Asia Minor, and first directed himself against the Rhodians, who had sided with Dolabella. They attempted to appease his wrath, but he declined to listen, and after defeating them by sea and by land, gained possession of the city, which he plundered. Plutarch relates that after his victory, when the Rhodians hailed him as king and lord, he replied: "Neither king nor lord, but the slayer and chastiser of the lord and king."[1]

Four objects are crowded together on the reverse of this coin; of these it is obvious that the *aplustre* alludes to victory at sea, while the diadem and the rose speak of the royal greeting which the Rhodians extended to their conqueror. But the crab is more difficult to explain. If the rose, as the Rhodian arms, alludes to the Rhodians, it would seem that the crab represents the arms of the neighbouring island of Cos.[2]

---

[1] Plut. *Brut.* 30.

[2] The crab had at this time almost disappeared from the Coan coinage; but, as it had from the earliest times been the standing type of the Coan coins, it doubtless always remained the badge or arms of the city.

HISTORICAL ROMAN COINS

It appears that Cassius's sea victory was won in Coan waters.[1] There is, indeed, just a possibility that the crab has not here any reference to Cos at all, but that, as Thalassa, the personification of the sea, wears a head-dress of crab's claws, so the crab may be a kind of short-hand for the sea. The reference to Cos, however, seems much less far-fetched.

Cassius's victory took place in 43 B.C. The coin itself was struck by his *legatus* M. Servilius, probably in the next year, after Cassius himself had left on the fatal expedition to Philippi; at any rate, after he had rejoined Brutus at Sardis, where he was saluted as imperator.

The form **CASSEI** on the obverse preserves an older form of the name, which was written with **EI** instead of **I**.

M. Servilius, the legate of Cassius, appears to be the person who was tribune of the people in 44 B.C., and was described by Cicero as *vir fortissimus*.[2]

THE LEGATES OF M. ANTONIUS IN GAUL.

42—41 B.C.

76. *Obv.* Female portrait bust r., with small wings on either side of neck.

---

[1] See Borghesi, *Œuvres*, i., p. 393; from Appian iv. 71. 300 f., we see that the action began off Myndus; cp. Cass. Dio, xlviii. 33.
[2] *Ad fam.* xii. 7; *Phil.* iv. 6, 16.

Rev. Lion walking r.; below and above [L]VGV
DVN[I]; in field l. [A], r. XL·

Silver *quinarius*. 1·43 grammes (22 grains). British Museum.

77. *Obv.* Similar to obv. of No. 76; around III.VIR·
R·P·C·

Rev. Similar to rev. of No. 76; above lion,
ANTONI, below IMP; in field l. A, r. XLI·

Silver *quinarius*. Cabinet des Médailles, Bibliothèque Nationale, Paris.

In the division of the provinces under the second triumvirate in 43 B.C., Lepidus received Spain and Gallia Narbonensis, Antonius the rest of Gaul. The two triumvirs were represented in their absence by legates; P. Ventidius Bassus seems to have governed Gallia Lugdunensis until, in 41 B.C., he left the province, which then came under Fufius Calenus.

M. Antonius was born in 82 B.C. His 40th birthday therefore fell in 42, his 41st in 41 B.C. Eckhel's interpretation of A XL and A XLI as *anni* or *annos xl.* or *xli.* has generally been accepted, the point of the commemoration of Antonius's age on these coins being clear if we assume, with Hirschfeld, that they were struck for his birthday and distributed to his troops.[1] The locative LVGVDVNI shows that the first, at any rate, was struck at Lugdunum. It is certainly odd that on the earlier *quinarii* the name of M. Antonius is not mentioned. But if they were distributed on his

---

[1] See above, on Caesar's coinage of 49 B.C. (p. 103).

birthday, everyone concerned must have known the meaning of the number **XL**. When the issue was repeated next year, we may suppose that the omission was rectified, and the name of Lugdunum had to give way to the name of the triumvir.

The types are significant. The woman who appears as Victory on the obverse is the triumvir's wife Fulvia. That is clear from a comparison with coins of the city of Eumeneia in Phrygia, which for a time bore after her the name of Fulvia; on those coins also she is represented as Victory. The lion on the reverse has been ingeniously interpreted [1] as the triumvir's genethliac sign. It appears from Pliny [2] that he showed the same sort of partiality for the lion as Augustus showed for the capricorn; and as the capricorn became the badge of several legions founded by Augustus, so, it has been thought, the lion was the badge of a legion established by M. Antonius. And as a matter of fact there exists a *quinarius* of Augustus with a running lion as its reverse type and the inscription **LEG. XVI**. It may well be, then, that this sixteenth legion was founded by M. Antonius, and that the *quinarii* struck at Lugdunum were issued for its especial benefit. But, whatever we may say as to

---

[1] By Willers, in the *Numism. Zeitschr.* xxxiv. (1902), in an elaborate study of the coinage of Lugdunum, to which the information given in the text is mainly due.

[2] *N. H.* viii. 21. 55.

these conjectures, there can be little doubt as to the occasion on which the coins were issued.

The early form Lugudunum for the name of the city is noteworthy.

SEXTUS POMPEIUS IN SICILY.
42—36 B.C.

78. *Obv.* Head of Sextus Pompeius r.; around, MAG· PIVS· IMP·ITER·; the whole in oak-wreath.

Rev. Heads of Cn. Pompeius Magnus r. and Cn. Pompeius the Younger l., confronted; on l., *lituus*, on r. tripod; above and below, PRAEF·CLAS·ET· ORAE MARIT·EX S·C· (some of the letters ligatured).

Aureus. 8·06 grammes (124·4 grains). British Museum.

79. *Obv.* The pharos of Messana; on the top, figure of Neptune (holding trident and dolphin, with his foot on a prow); lying before it, a war-galley, bearing a military eagle, a trident and a thyrsos. Around, inscription as on obv. of No. 78.

Rev. Scylla, with double tail, and foreparts of wolves around her waist, brandishing an oar; around, inscription as on rev. of No. 78.

Silver *denarius*. 3·86 grammes (59·5 grains). British Museum.

Sextus Pompeius Magnus was the younger son of

HISTORICAL ROMAN COINS

Pompeius the Great. From the time of the battle of Pharsalia he was almost continuously a thorn in the side of Caesar, and, after the dictator's death, of Antonius and Octavian. In 44 B.C., when the Senate broke with M. Antonius, Pompeius was appointed praefect of the fleet and of the sea-coast, as he calls himself on his coins. The phrase **EX S·C·** which follows the title refers, probably, to the grant of this office, and not to the grant of the right of coinage. From the beginning of the triumvirate, being proscribed, he turned pirate, and eventually (in 42 B.C.) made himself master of Sicily. Here he held out for six years, until Agrippa, defeating him first at Mylae and then decisively at Naulochus, broke his power. He fled to the East, where he met his death in 35 B.C. During his six years in Sicily his only idea seems to have been to annoy the triumvirs, without aspiring to restore the Republican *régime* or to seize the supreme power himself. His rough, uncultured nature[1] is well expressed in the portrait on the obverse of his *aureus*. As the avenger of his father and his elder brother (killed in Spain after the battle of Munda in 45), he calls himself "Pius," and represents their portraits on his coinage. The *denarius* is one of a number with types of local interest: for all these coins appear to

[1] Vell. Paterc. ii. 73: hic adolescens erat studiis rudis, sermone barbarus, impetu strenuus, manu promtus, cogitatione celer, fide patri dissimillimus, libertorum suorum libertus, servorumque servus, speciosis invidens, ut pareret humillimis.

have been struck in Sicily.¹ Scylla symbolizes the Straits of Messana; the obverse of the same coin shows an admiral's galley² occupying the harbour of Messana. On the pharos is a statue of Neptune, naturally appropriate to such a place, but also significant of the fact that Sextus claimed to be "son of Neptune." He called himself *Imperator iterum*, probably after his defeat of Q. Salvidienus Rufus in 42 B.C.; a victory over Asinius Pollio in Spain in 45 or 44 having allowed him to take the title for the first time.³

The augurship of Pompeius the Great⁴ is alluded to by the *lituus* behind his head; the tripod is also the symbol of some priestly office.

Q. LABIENUS PARTHICUS.
40 B.C.

80. *Obv.* Head of Labienus r.; around, Q. LABIENVS ΓARTHICVS IMΓ.

Rev. Bridled and saddled horse standing r.

Silver *denarius*. 3·78 grammes (58·3 grains). British Museum.

---

[1] For others see my *Coins of Ancient Sicily*, Pl. xv. 6 and 9.
[2] The meaning of the thyrsos which leans against the *aplustre* (or stern ornament) is obscure. It is found in the same position on the ship in the beautiful Ludovisi relief representing Paris and Oenone. Attempts have been made to explain the significance of this Dionysiac emblem on the relief, but without success. It seems still more out of place on the flagship of Sextus Pompeius.
[3] Cassius Dio, xlv. 10.
[4] Cic. *Phil.* ii. 4.

HISTORICAL ROMAN COINS

Q. Labienus[1] was the son of that T. Labienus who, after serving under Caesar in Gaul, deserted to the side of Pompeius, and was slain at Munda. After the murder of Caesar, Quintus was sent to Parthia by Brutus and Cassius to obtain help from King Orodes; and he stayed in the country until, in 40 B.C., a favourable opportunity occurred for him to strike a blow against the power of the triumvirs. With Pacorus, the son of Orodes, he invaded Syria, which for the most part submitted without a blow. Leaving Pacorus to complete the work in Syria, Labienus overran the greater part of southern Asia Minor, reaching as far as Caria. His successes induced him to take the title of *Parthicus Imperator*, which must have been doubly offensive to a Western ear, since, according to Roman usage, it should have meant that he was the conqueror of the Parthians, not their ally. The orator Hybreas, who unsuccessfully defended the Carian fortress of Mylasa against him, ironically proposed to call himself Καρικὸς αὐτοκράτωρ.[2] The successes of Labienus in

---

[1] Labienus is a gentile name, but the error which regards it as a cognomen of the *gens Atia* still persists. For the career of Labienus, see especially Cassius Dio, xlviii. 24—26, 39, 40.

[2] Strabo, xiv. 660. Strictly speaking, no doubt, "Parthicus" and "imperator" are co-ordinate words, qualifying "Q. Labienus." But Hybreas chose to take "Parthicus" as an adjective qualifying "imperator"; or perhaps he knew no better. Cassius Dio carefully says αὐτοκράτορά τε αὐτὸν καὶ Παρθικόν γε ἐκ τοῦ ἐναντιωτάτου τοῖς Ῥωμαίοις ἔθους ὠνόμαζεν (liv. 26). Gardthausen (*Augustus* I. i., p. 225) seems to have missed the point of Hybreas' joke.

Asia Minor were brought to a close by M. Antonius' lieutenant, P. Ventidius, in 39 B.C.

The coin of Labienus must have been issued by him either in Syria (at some such place as Antioch) or in Asia Minor. A Syrian mint is, on the whole, more probable, although it cannot reasonably be argued from a statement of Cassius Dio that Labienus took no Parthian cavalry with him across the Taurus.[1] Labienus doubtless claimed that he was issuing money in virtue of his Roman *imperium*; so he issued it of the weight and in the style of the *denarius*; and, at the same time, struck an *aureus* precisely like it in all respects save metal and weight.

The reverse type alludes to the Parthian light cavalry with which he raided Roman territory. It offers an admirable contrast to the conventional representation of horses which prevails at this time, is evidently carefully studied from the life, and gives a better idea than anything else now extant of what the Parthian horse was like. It is difficult to explain what it is that hangs from the saddle. One of the Scythian horses on a famous silver vase, from Tchertomlitsk in South Russia,[2] carries an object depending from its saddle in the same way, but on a much smaller scale. None of the explanations that

[1] XLVIII. 39: when Ventidius came upon Labienus in Asia Minor, Labienus ἄνευ τῶν Πάρθων μετὰ τῶν αὐτόθεν στρατιωτῶν μόνων ἦν.

[2] Kondakoff, Tolstoi and Reinach, *Antiquités de la Russie Méridionale*, p. 298. I owe this analogy to Mr. O. M. Dalton.

occur to the mind (bow-case, stirrup, saddle-bag, saddle-cloth) seems satisfactory.

Ventidius, says Dio,[1] got nothing from the Senate for his services, because he was serving merely as Antonius' lieutenant. A rare *denarius*, on which both Antonius and Ventidius are named with the title *imp(erator)*, has been associated with the campaign of Ventidius against Labienus and the Parthians. It was, however, more probably issued in Cisalpine Gaul when Ventidius was acting on behalf of Antonius in 43 B.C., or else a little later, during the Perusine War. M. Antonius is still represented as wearing a beard in mourning for Julius Caesar. There is no numismatic record of Ventidius' Parthian victories.[2]

THE ARMENIAN EXPEDITION OF M. ANTONIUS.

34 B.C.

81. *Obv.* Head of M. Antonius r.; around, AN-TONIVS · AVGVR· COS · DES · ITER · ET · TERT.

Rev. Armenian tiara, with bow and arrow (or sceptre) crossed behind it; around, IMP TERTIO III VIR · R · P · C.

Silver *denarius*. Cabinet des Médailles, Bibliothèque Nationale, Paris.

---

[1] XLVIII. 41. He was compensated, however, when Antonius sent him back to Rome, by a splendid triumph in Nov. 38, after which he disappears from history.

[2] Except probably the dates on coins of Rhosus; see *Journ. Internat. d'Arch. Num.* 1903, pp. 47 f.

HISTORICAL ROMAN COINS

82. *Obv.* Bust of Cleopatra r., diademed, with small prow before it; around, CLEO[PATRAE REGINAE] REGVM FILIORVM REGVM.

Rev. Head of M. Antonius r.; behind, small Armenian tiara; around, ANTONI · [A]RMEN[IA] · DEVICTA.

Silver *denarius*. 3·58 grammes (55·2 grains). British Museum.

On his unfortunate expedition against the Parthian Phraates in 36 B.C., M. Antonius was accompanied by his ally Artavasdes, King of Armenia, with 6,000 horse and 7,000 foot. But, after the destruction of the Roman siege-train under Oppius Statianus, Artavasdes deserted the Roman cause, and returned to Armenia with his troops. As the king was thus in some measure responsible for the subsequent disasters to the Roman forces, Antonius determined to have his revenge; but he concealed his intentions until after his return to Syria. In the spring of 34 B.C. he invaded Armenia, obtained possession of the person of Artavasdes by treachery, and carried him off to figure in the triumph which was celebrated at Alexandria. The recognition of the eastern capital as a place where an imperator could triumph as well as in Rome earned for Antonius no small unpopularity. At the same time he proclaimed Cleopatra Queen of Egypt, Cyprus, Libya, and Coele-Syria; her sons received the title of King of Kings, Armenia with other kingdoms being assigned to Alexander, while Cleopatra herself was hailed as "Queen of Kings."[1]

Antonius was designated consul for the second and third time in 39 B.C.[2] His third imperatorship dates from 39,[3] or at latest from 36 B.C. (the Parthian expedition being regarded by courtesy as victorious),[4] and his second consulship from 34 B.C. The *denarius* No. 81, on which he is described as "imperator tertio" but is not yet "cos. ii.," must have been struck at the latest in 35 B.C. Now in this year Antonius had not even started on his Armenian expedition. The Armenian tiara that forms the type of the reverse is evidently therefore an anticipation of the subjection of the country.[5] The coins were probably struck at Alexandria during the preparations for the expedition which started in the next spring. On the other hand, the *denarius* with the head of Cleopatra, describing her as "Queen of Kings, the sons of Kings," was doubtless issued after the return of M. Antonius to Alexandria with Artavasdes in his train. Accordingly

[1] Cass. Dio, xlix. 41.

[2] Babelon, i., p. 160.

[3] Supposing that he was acclaimed imperator on the strength of Ventidius' defeats of Labienus and the Parthians.

[4] We know that Antonius sent to Rome announcements of imaginary successes in this campaign (Cass. Dio, xlix. 32).

[5] As Mr. Grueber reminds me, Antonius promised at this time to give Lesser Armenia to Polemo I. of Pontus, as a reward for the mission on which he sent him to the Median king. He kept his word (Cass. Dio, xlix. 33, 44). Mr. Grueber thinks that it is this claim to dispose of Lesser Armenia which is illustrated by our coin.

we have the tiara behind the conqueror's head, and the inscription **ARMENIA DEVICTA**. The prow, which appears as an adjunct to the portrait of Cleopatra, is difficult to explain, unless it be the mark of some Syrian mint, such as Tripolis or Berytus.

OCTAVIAN'S TRIUMPH.

29 B.C.

83. *Obv.* Victory to r. on prow of galley, holding wreath in r. and palm-branch in l.

Rev. Octavian in a triumphal quadriga r., holding laurel-branch ; in exergue, **CAESAR DIVI F.**

Silver *denarius.* 3·78 grammes (58·3 grains). B.M.C. II., p. 12, No. 4342.

84. *Obv.* Similar to preceding.

Rev. Similar to preceding, but with inscription replaced by **IMP · CAESAR**.

Silver *denarius.* 3·98 grammes (61·4 grains). B.M.C. II., p. 13, No. 4343.

The triple triumph which Octavian celebrated on his return from the East in the summer of 29 B.C. is alluded to in various ways on the coinage of the time. The victory of Actium in particular is commemorated not merely by the type of Victory on a prow, but also by a figure of Neptune standing with one foot on a globe, and by a combined naval and military trophy. The Neptune and the Victory are interesting as showing a conscious adaptation of types used by Demetrius Poliorcetes on his coinage to commemorate his victory over Ptolemy in 306 B.C. The Greek, on one of his coins, represented Poseidon standing with his foot on a rock, leaning with his left hand on his trident—probably a reproduction of a statue. On another was Victory, blowing a trumpet, on a prow— this too representing a statue, which is still preserved to us in the Victory of Samothrace in the Louvre. Octavian makes Neptune (or perhaps himself in the guise of the god) stand with his foot on a globe, and hold an *aplustre*; he rests with his left hand on a trident, but he wears a sword at his side! His Victory, instead of the magnificent figure of the fourth-century artist, is a wreath-and-palm-bearing winged woman of highly conventional style. The types thus show, not merely a conscious adaptation, but a frigid modification of a great original.

It will be noticed that the two *denarii* here described differ only in the legend of the reverse. The coins on which Octavian is called *Imperator Caesar* (No. 84) appear to date from the years 29 to 27 B.C. In the latter year he received the title *Augustus*. The coin with *Caesar Divi filius* (No. 83), on the other hand, is one of a class which is assigned to the period 36 to 29 B.C. Since it refers to the Actian triumph, it must belong to the very end of this period.

Octavian was saluted as imperator twenty-one times

in all, the first occasion being in 43 B.C. But he also employed the word, and does so here, in an extraordinary sense, in that he used it as a personal praenomen, inheritable by his children, and having no direct reference to military achievements. When he assumed this praenomen in 29 B.C.,[1] he dropped his old praenomen Gaius.

CAESAR AUGUSTUS.

27 B.C.

85. *Obv.* Head of Augustus r.; around, **CAESAR· COS· VII· CIVIBVS· SERVATEIS.**

Rev. An eagle, wings spread, holding in his talons an oak-wreath; behind his wings, two branches of laurel; above, **AVGVSTVS**; at sides of wreath, **S· C.**

<small>*Aureus.* 7·81 grammes (120·5 grains). B.M.C. II., p. 18, No. 4371.</small>

86. *Obv.* Head of Augustus r; around, **CAESAR AVGVSTVS·**

Rev. A shield, inscribed **S·P·Q·R·CL·V·**, leaning against a column; before the column, Victory flying r., holding in her hands a wreath.

<small>*Aureus.* 7·92 grammes (122·2 grains). B.M.C. II., p. 22, No. 4385.</small>

In the Will of Augustus we read: senatu[s consulto Aug(ustus) appe]llatus sum et laureis postes

---

[1] Cass. Dio, lii. 41; cp. xliii. 44.

HISTORICAL ROMAN COINS

aedium mearum v[estiti publice coronaq]ue civica super ianuam meam fixa est [clupeusque aureu]s in [c]uria Iulia positus, quem mihi senatum [populumque Romanu]m dare virtutis clem[entia]e iustitia[e pietatis causa testatum] est pe[r e]ius clupei [inscription]em.[1]

The title of Augustus was conferred on Octavian on 16th January, 727 (= 27 B.C.) by decree of the Senate. Three days earlier the honours of the oaken crown and the laurels at his door had been granted to him. Cassius Dio tells us[2] that laurel trees were placed before the door of the house of Octavian, and an oak-wreath hung above it. This is confirmed by a coin of L. Caninius Gallus, which shows a pair of laurel trees and an oak-wreath in position at the door of the Emperor's house.

The golden shield of valour mentioned in the will is described in an inscription[3] in the following words: S.P.Q.R. Augusto dedit clupeum virtutis [c]le[men]-ti[ae ius]t[itiae pietatis causa]. Ancient writers are silent regarding it. But there can be little doubt that it was voted to the Emperor at the same time as the other decorations. It was deposited, as Augustus tells us, in the Senate House, where also stood the statue of Victory from Tarentum, with the altar which he dedicated in the year 29. This fact is illustrated

---

[1] *Mon. Anc.* (Mommsen, *Res Gestae Divi Aug.*) c. 34.
[2] LIII. 16.
[3] *C. I. L.* ix. 5809. Other inscriptions also refer to it.

in the type of the coin No. 86, which connects Victory with the shield of valour. On the preceding coin the oaken *corona civica* is borne by an eagle. This is the symbol of Empire, which Augustus is said to have borrowed from Egypt, where it had, almost from the foundation of the Ptolemaic dynasty, been used on the coins as the type of sovereignty.[1] It must, however, be remembered that the Romans had long used the eagle for the purposes of a standard in war; and, the Empire being based on a military imperium, the bird would naturally come to be used as its emblem.

Count de Salis assigned the *aureus* with the eagle to the year 27 B.C., and the other piece before us to the period 24—20 B.C. His reasons for this division appear to lie in the treatment of the portrait. For our purpose, it is sufficient to note that both were struck between 27 and 20 B.C., and that No. 86, with its pointed reference to the decree of 16th January, 27, was doubtless issued in that very year.

THE RECOVERY OF THE STANDARDS.

20 B.C.

87. *Obv.* Head of Augustus r.; below, [AVGVSTVS]. Linear border.

Rev. **SIGNIS PARTHICIS RECEPTIS** in three lines, within a linear circle.

Silver *denarius*. 3·82 grammes (59 grains). British Museum.

---

[1] See Oder in Pauly-Wissowa, *Realencycl.* i. 375.

HISTORICAL ROMAN COINS

88. *Obv.* Head of Augustus r; around, **CAESAR AVGVSTVS**.

Rev. Mars, nude but for a slight cloak fastened round his waist, helmeted, walking to l., looking back; he holds in his right a legionary eagle, in his left the standard of a maniple; inscription on l. **SIGNIS**, on r. **RECEPTIS**.

Silver *denarius*. 4·36 grammes (67·3 grains). B.M.C. II., p. 26, No. 4405.

89. *Obv.* Head of Augustus r.; around, **S·P·Q·R· IMP· CAESARI· AVG· COS· XI· TR· POT· VI.**

Rev. Triumphal arch with three openings; above, Augustus in quadriga to front, between a Parthian (on l.), offering a manipular standard, and another (on r.), offering a legionary eagle and holding in his l. a bow; around, **CIVIB·ET·SIGN· MILIT·A·PART·RECVP·**.

Aureus. 7·81 grammes (120·5 grains). B.M.C. II., p. 37, No. 4453.

90. *Obv.* Head of Augustus l.; around, **CAESAR AVGVSTVS**.

Rev. Circular domed temple; within, Mars to l., holding a legionary eagle and a manipular standard; across the field, **MAR VLT**.

Silver *denarius*. 3·89 grammes (60·0 grains). B.M.C. II., p. 28, No. 4411.

The stroke of diplomacy by which in 20 B.C.

Augustus induced Phraates to return the standards which the Parthians had on three different occasions captured from Roman armies was one of the achievements of which he was most proud. "Signa militaria complur[a per] alios d[u]ces ami[ssa] devicti[s hostibus reciperavi] ex Hispania et [Gallia et a Dalm]ateis. Parthos trium exercitum Roman[o]rum spolia et signa re[ddere] mihi supplicesque amicitiam populi Romani petere coegi. ea autem si[gn]a in penetrali, quod e[s]t in templo Martis Ultoris, reposui."[1] The standards recovered from the Dalmatians (in 33 B.C.) were those which had been lost in 48 by Gabinius and in 44 by Vatinius. Of those recovered from Spaniards and Gauls we know no more than Augustus tells us. The three armies defeated by the Parthians were those commanded by Crassus (in 53), and by the legates of M. Antonius,—L. Decidius Saxa in 40, and Oppius Statianus in 36. The Parthians, threatened by Augustus with war, handed over to Tiberius the standards which they had retained, as well as some prisoners.[2] Augustus celebrated their recovery with great pomp; among other things, he erected the triumphal arch which is represented on the *aureus* No. 89. The standards themselves were placed in the temple of Mars the Avenger. By this, in the passage

---

[1] *Mon. Anc.* c. 29. Cp. Cassius Dio (liv. 8): ἐφρόνει μέγα, λέγων ὅτι τὰ πρότερόν ποτε ἐν ταῖς μάχαις ἀπολόμενα ἀκονιτὶ ἐκεκόμιστο.

[2] Sueton. *Divus Aug.* 21; *Tib.* 9; Cass. Dio, liv. 8.

quoted from the Will of Augustus, is undoubtedly meant the Temple in the Forum of Augustus. But as that was not finished until the year 2 B.C., the standards must have been placed elsewhere in the meantime. A small shrine of the god was erected on the Capitol in 20 B.C., and it is definitely stated by Cassius Dio[1] that it was meant for the reception of the standards. Both Horace and Propertius, however, seem to imply that they were dedicated to Jupiter:

> Tua, Caesar, aetas . . .
> signa nostro restituit Iovi
> derepta Parthorum superbis
> postibus.
> (Hor. *Carm.* iv. 16. 6.)

> Adsuescent Latio Partha tropaea Iovi.
> (Prop. iii. (iv.) 4. 6.)

It is accordingly tempting to assume that they found a temporary resting-place in the Temple of Jupiter on the Capitol. But, on the other hand, we have the definite assertion of Dio just cited. At first sight it would appear that the passages of Horace and Propertius cannot be regarded as good evidence against the statement of the historian. But they are not really contradictory. The historian only says that Augustus decreed the erection of a temple on this occasion; but the standards must have been kept somewhere pending its completion. Has the temple of Jupiter Feretrius more claim to consideration as the

[1] LIV. 8.

temporary resting-place of the standards than the small shrine of Mars Ultor on the Capitol? Let us examine the coins.

Of the few coins chosen here, out of the many which commemorate this achievement, the first (No. 87) was struck in the East, possibly at Pergamum.[1] The second (No. 88), on the other hand, is of Roman fabric. The war-god carries a legionary eagle in one hand, a manipular standard in the other. Both kinds of standards are, of course, included in the general term *signum*. This coin was probably struck on the return of Augustus to Rome in 19 B.C. These pieces do not assist us to decide the question of the temples. But on No. 90 (also struck in Rome at the same time as No. 88), we see a circular-domed temple of Mars Ultor.

Now Borghesi[2] and Mommsen[3] regard this type as an anticipatory representation of the greater temple eventually dedicated in the Forum of Augustus. There is, of course, nothing improbable in the suggestion that the type should thus anticipate the completion of the temple which had been vowed during the campaign of Philippi.[4] But one thing is very clear from the remains of the temple itself, and that is that it was not circular, but an octastyle

---

[1] E. Gabrici, *Numism. di Augusto* in Milani's *Studi e Materiali*, ii.
[2] *Œuvres*, ii., p. 379.
[3] *Res gest. div. Aug.* p. 126.
[4] See *supra*, p. 114. n. 1.

HISTORICAL ROMAN COINS

peripteros.[1] Obviously then, either the representation, if it is meant for the temple in the Forum of Augustus, is quite imaginary, or else the original plans were completely altered when it came to building. But neither alternative is so reasonable as the supposition that in the temple on the coins of 19 B.C. we have the shrine which Augustus built on the Capitol, hard by the temple of Jupiter Feretrius, as a temporary resting-place to receive the standards until they should be transferred to a more permanent abode.[2]

This being so, the references by Horace and Propertius to Jupiter must be taken in a general sense, as indicating merely that the standards were placed on the Capitol, which was especially associated with Jupiter.

THE PROVINCE OF ASIA.
19 B.C.

91. *Obv.* Head of Augustus r.; below, IMP·IX·TR·PO·V.

Rev. Façade of a hexastyle temple, inscribed on architrave ROM·ET·AVGVST; across field, COM ASIAE.

Silver "cistophoric medallion." 11·92 grammes (184 grains). British Museum.

The date of this piece is fixed, by the titles given to Augustus on the obverse, to 19 B.C. The coin

---

[1] See, for instance, the plan in Lanciani, *Ruins and Excavations*, p. 305.
[2] So Richter in Baumeister's *Denkmäler*, iii. p. 1480; A. Schneider, *das alte Rom*, Pl. viii. 12.

itself is one of a class[1] which corresponded in weight and purpose to the *cistophori* which had long been the chief silver currency of the province of Asia.[2] The old cistophoric types gradually disappeared; thus on a piece issued in the name of M. Antonius, about 39—38 B.C., the ivy-wreath, snakes and *cista mystica* still remain, but on the obverse we have the head of M. Antonius in the wreath, while the *cista* is transferred to the reverse, where with the head of Octavia it occupies the place of the old bow-case. On a piece of Octavian, struck in 28 B.C., the only relic of the old types is the *cista*, used as an adjunct in the field of the reverse.

Although it was no new thing for the different cities of a province to send representatives to a common assembly for some definite purpose, Augustus is rightly credited with having first organized the Κοινὸν Ἀσίας (*commune Asiae*) in the form which it was to maintain for nearly three centuries. The assembly met periodically, and its object was above all to celebrate the joint cult of Rome and Augustus. Once their religious functions had been fulfilled, the members could proceed to deliberate on matters of politics interesting the province. In the province of Asia there was one supreme high priest of this cult,

---

[1] On which see E. Gabrici, *Numism. di Augusto*, in Milani's *Studi e Materiali*, ii.
[2] *Hist. Gr. Coins*, p. 138 f.

known simply as ἀρχιερεύς Ἀσίας. In addition, however, there were a certain number of ἀρχιερεῖς Ἀσίας, each of whom was attached to the temple of the Κοινόν in the various cities which possessed such temples: thus we have an ἀρχιερεὺς Ἀσίας ναῶν τῶν ἐν Περγάμῳ. Pergamum, indeed, was the first city in which a temple of Rome and Augustus was erected at the expense of the province; and it is probably this Pergamene temple that is represented on our coin. Not improbably also the occasion for the issue of this, and other coins connected with it, was the dedication of the temple.[1] Other cities at which the assembly is known to have met are Ephesus, Smyrna, Sardis, Cyzicus, Laodicea and Philadelphia. This provincial cult was the focus of the official religion of the provinces during the first three centuries of the Empire, and its importance cannot be exaggerated as a public expression of the relations between the provinces and Rome. Its organization was one of the most masterly achievements of Augustus.

ARMENIA RECEPTA.
CIRCA 19 B.C.

92. *Obv.* Head of Augustus r.; below, **AVGVST[VS]**.
Rev. Armenian tiara, bow-case with bow and quiver with arrows; above and below, **ARMENIA RECEPTA**.

Silver *denarius*. 3·76 grammes (58 grains).   British Museum.

[1] Gabrici, *op. cit.* p. 15.

HISTORICAL ROMAN COINS

Artaxias, who succeeded to the throne of Armenia, when his father Artavasdes was taken prisoner by M. Antonius in 34 B.C., had a troubled reign of some 14 years. His brother Tigranes, who had also fallen into the hands of Antonius, had passed into the possession of Augustus. When Augustus was in the East, actually preparing an expedition against Artaxias,[1] the Armenians begged that Tigranes might be sent back to rule over them. While the young prince was on his way, conducted by Tiberius, Artaxias was murdered by his subjects. " Armeniam maiorem," says Augustus in his Will,[2] " interfecto rege eius Artaxe c[u]m possem facere provinciam, malui maiorum nostrorum exemplo regn[u]m id Tigrani regis Artavasdis filio, nepoti autem Tigranis regis, per T[i. Ne]ronem trad[er]e, qui tum mihi priv[ig]nus erat. et eandem gentem postea d[esc]iscentem et rebellantem domit[a]m per Gaium filium meum regi Ario[barz]ani regis Medorum Artaba[zi] filio regendam tradidi et post e[ius] mortem filio eius Artavasdi. quo [inte]rfecto [Tigra]ne(m), qui erat ex regio genere Armeniorum oriundus, in id re[gnum] misi."

The *denarius* before us is generally supposed

---

[1] On this sojourn in the East, see Gabrici, *Il secondo Viaggio di Augusto in Oriente*, Naples, 1900, and the same writer's *Numismatica di Augusto* in Milani's *Studi e Materiali*, ii.

[2] *Mon. Anc.* c. 27; cp. Tac. *Ann.* ii. 3; Vell. Paterc. ii. 94; Cass. Dio, liv. 9.

HISTORICAL ROMAN COINS

to refer to the occasion when Tiberius occupied Armenia in force, and the country accepted a king at the hands of Augustus. The fabric of the coin shows that it was struck in the East; and there is much to be said for the suggestion that the mint was Pergamum, and the occasion the dedication of the temple of Rome and Augustus which had been begun nine years earlier.[1]

The types explain themselves: the bow and arrows of the Armenian soldiery, and the Armenian royal tiara,[2] a tall head-dress with dentated crown. The latter varies in some details from the tiara worn by Tigranes the Great on his coins[3]—that, for instance, has flaps hanging down on to the shoulders—but in general form it is the same.

Some of the coins commemorating the events in Armenia use, instead of "recepta," the form "capta." It is possible that the coins with "recepta" are the earlier, and that the form "capta" was an afterthought, for "recepta" recalled the fact of the previous subjugation of Armenia by M. Antonius, whose exploits it was not to the purpose of Augustus to glorify.[4]

---

[1] Gabrici, *Numism. di Augusto*, p. 15.
[2] Cp. the coins of M. Antonius, above, No. 81.
[3] *Hist. Gr. Coins*, Pl. xiii. 96.
[4] Gabrici, *op. cit.*, p. 12.

HISTORICAL ROMAN COINS

THE SECULAR GAMES.

17 B.C.

93. *Obv.* Head of Augustus r. laureate; around, IMP· CAESAR TR·POT·IIX·

Rev. Augustus seated l. on a platform inscribed LVD·S; he hands an object, taken from a basket at his feet, to one of two togate figures standing before him; in exergue, AVG·SVF·P; around, [L·ME]CSI NIVS.

Aureus. 8·01 grammes (123·6 grains). B.M.C. II., p. 53, No. 4487.

94. *Obv.* Head of Augustus r. laureate; around CAE [SAR] AVGVSTVS·TR POT·

Rev. A cippus inscribed IMP CAES AVG LVD SAEC; across field, $\overline{\text{XV}}$ S·F; around [L· MESCIN]IVS RVFVS [III·VIR].

Silver *denarius.* 3·47 grammes (53·5 grains). B.M.C. II., p. 54, No. 4488.

Since Augustus is described on the former of these coins as holding the tribunician power for the eighth time, its date is fixed to the year 16 B.C. We know nothing of the moneyer L. Mescinius Rufus; for there is some difficulty in identifying him with the man of that name who was Cicero's quaestor in Cilicia in 51, and served under Cassius in Asia in 43. Augustus, as master of the college of *quindecimviri sacris faciundis*, celebrated the secular games for the college in the consulship of C. Furnius and C. Silanus,[1] *i.e.*, in 17 B.C., the year preceding the issue of the coins of Mescinius. The letters X̄V̄ S·F· on No. 94 are probably to be taken as referring to Augustus, *xvvir sacris faciundis*, rather than to the whole college of *xvviri*. They were, as a matter of fact, for this special occasion at least twenty-one in number, and their names are preserved.[2] Augustus, in the Monumentum Ancyranum, mentions Agrippa as his colleague. Agrippa, nevertheless, was not one of the five *magistri* of the college, whose names are preserved elsewhere.[3]

Before the games began, the *quindecimviri*, seated on platforms, distributed to the people purificatories for fumigation. These were known as *purgamenta* or *suffimenta*, and their distribution is illustrated on the reverse of No. 93, with the inscription *Aug(ustus) suf(fimenta) p(opulo dedit)*. The purification was effected by the burning of torches with sulphur and bitumen; only after this had been done were the people fit to partake in the festival.

Other features of the festival are alluded to on other coins of Augustus. Thus, on *aurei* and *denarii* of M. Sanquinius, dating from 12 B.C., there is represented the herald who proclaimed the festival; he wears a helmet decorated with two long plumes, and

---

[1] *Mon. Anc.* ch. xxii. Mommsen, *Res gest.*, pp. 91 f.
[2] *Eph. Epigr.* viii. pp. 240 ff.
[3] Fasti Capitolini, *C. I. L.* i. p. 442.

HISTORICAL ROMAN COINS

carries a caduceus and a circular shield. On other pieces, probably struck in the year of the games, two priests (perhaps Augustus with another person) are occupied in sacrifice at the altar. Further light is thrown on the various ceremonies by the coinage of Domitian, who celebrated the secular games for the sixth time in his fourteenth consulship (A.D. 88).[1]

THE PUBLIC ROADS.
17 B.C.

95. *Obv.* Head of Augustus r. ; around, S·P·Q·R·IMP· CAESARI.

Rev. Triumphal arch with two openings on a viaduct or bridge; on the arch, Augustus, crowned by Victory, standing in a car drawn by two elephants; around, QVOD VIAE MVN·SVNT.

Aureus. 7·83 grammes (120·8 grains). B.M.C. II., p. 39, No. 4462.

96. *Obv.* Head of Augustus r.; around, AVGVSTVS TR·POT·VII·

Rev. On a cippus, the inscription [S·P·]Q·R· | IMP· CAE | QVOD V· | M·S·EX· | EAP·Q·IS | AD A·DE ; around, L·VINICIVS L· [F·IIIVIR].

Silver *denarius.* 4·03 grammes (62·2 grains). B.M.C. II., p. 49, No. 4471.

[1] The whole of the material relating to the history of the secular games has been collected by Mommsen and Dressel in *Eph. Epigr.* viii. pp. 225—315, and by O. Wasiner, *Ludi Saeculares* (Warsaw, 1901, in Russian).

HISTORICAL ROMAN COINS

The restoration of the great Italian roads is one of the most important public works which stand to the credit of Augustus. In his Will[1] he records that in his seventh consulship (*i.e.*, 727 A.U.C. = 27 B.C.) he restored the Flaminian Way from the city to Ariminum, and all the bridges except the Mulvian and the Minucian. An inscription on the arch at Ariminum records that it was erected in honour of Augustus, "v[ia flamin]ia [et reliquei]s celeberrimeis Italiae vieis consilio [et sumptib]us [eius mu]niteis."[2] Further, we know from Cassius Dio[3] that in commemoration of the work statues of Augustus were set up on the bridge over the Tiber and in Ariminum.

The inscription on the second of our two coins is to be expanded: S(enatus) p(opulus)q(ue) R(omanus) Imp(eratori) Caes(ari) quod v(iae) m(unitae) s(unt) ex ea p(ecunia) q(uam) is ad a(erarium) de(tulit). This must be one of the four occasions mentioned by Augustus in his Will (chap. 17), in which he came to the assistance of the treasury. Mommsen[4] draws a distinction between money thus given by Augustus out of his private purse, and money obtained by the sale of booty (*manubiae*) and devoted to public works. It was out of such *pecunia manubialis* that the Temple of

---

[1] Ch. 20; Mommsen, *Res gest.* p. 86.
[2] Cf. Suet. *Aug.* 30.
[3] LIII. 22.
[4] *Op. cit.* p. 66.

Mars Ultor was built,[1] and the Flaminian Way restored.[2] It would follow, if Mommsen is right, that the grant made by Augustus to the treasury, and commemorated on the cippus on No. 96, was not identical with the money expended by him on the Flaminian Way. However this may be—and the distinction appears to be somewhat over-subtle—it seems probable that the triumphal arch erected on a viaduct or bridge, represented on No. 95, is one of those erected on the Flaminian Way. Whether it is the arch on the Mulvian bridge (the bridge over the Tiber mentioned by Dio), or some other, we can hardly decide. But it can scarcely be meant for the arch at Rimini, which has but a single opening. And the road on which it stands looks more like a viaduct than a bridge.

In any case, the *aureus*, No. 95, commemorating though it does an event of 27 B.C., was nevertheless not struck until ten years later; for it belongs to a class which are assignable on various good grounds to 17 B.C. The *denarius*, No. 96, again, is dated by the fact that Augustus held the *tribunicia potestas* for the seventh time in 17—16 B.C.[3]

We may assume that the year 17 B.C. saw the

---

[1] *Mon. Anc.* ch. xxi.

[2] Suet. *Aug.* 30 : desumpta sibi Flaminia via Arimino tenus munienda reliquas triumphalibus viris e manubiali pecunia sternendas distribuit.

[3] Another coin of Vinicius is dated TR. POT. VIII., *i.e.*, in 16 B.C., but late in the year.

completion of the work of restoring the roads which had been begun in 27 B.C. Probably the Flaminian Way was finished early in the period; but when the general completion of the works was commemorated the road especially associated with Augustus naturally figured on the coins.

Other triumphal arches are commemorated on coins of the same date. Thus we have one resembling in every particular that already described, except that the car of Augustus is drawn by four horses. There is another (see No. 89) of quite a different character associated with the recovery of the standards (**CIVIB· ET·SIGN·MILIT·A·PART·RECVP·**). Of these probably only the former belonged to the Flaminian Way.

THE MONETARY REFORM OF AUGUSTUS.
CIRCA 15 B.C.

97. *Obv.* Oak wreath between two laurel-branches; inscription **OB CIVIS SERVATOS**.

Rev. The letters **S·C** surrounded by the inscription **C·CASSIVS·C·F·CELER·IIIVIR. A·A·A·F·F.**

Brass *sestertius*. 27·11 grammes (418·4 grains). B.M.C. II., p. 58, No. 4501.

98. *Obv.* Oak wreath; inscription **AVGVSTVS TRIBVNIC POTEST.**

Rev. Similar to No. 97, but without **C·F**.

Brass *dupondius*. 8·28 grammes (127·8 grains). B.M.C. II., p. 59, No. 4505.

HISTORICAL ROMAN COINS

99. *Obv.* Head of Augustus r. ; around, CAESAR AVGVSTVS TRIBVNIC POTEST.

Rev. Similar to No. 97, but without C·F.

Copper *as.* 11·15 grammes (172·0 grains). B.M.C. II., p. 59, No. 4507.

100. *Obv.* Cornucopiae between S C ; around, PVLCHER·TAVRVS·REGVLVS.

Rev. Coin anvil, wreathed ; around, III·VIR· A·A·A·F·F.

Copper *quadrans.* 3·37 grammes (52·1 grains). B.M.C. II., p. 76, No. 4577.

The four coins represent the four denominations which were instituted by Augustus. The *quadrans* was never issued in large quantities; but the three higher denominations persisted for nearly three centuries. To modern eyes, time having covered the surfaces of the majority of coins with a deceptive patina, the distinction between the *dupondius* and the *as* is usually imperceptible. But from analysis, combined with a statement of Pliny,[1] we know that the *sestertius* and the *dupondius* were of brass and the *as* and the *quadrans*[2] of copper. The denominations, as will be seen from Nos. 97—100, are

[1] *H. N.* xxxiv. 2. 4: the copper of Corduba contains, after that of the Livian mines, the greatest proportion of zinc and equals the quality of *orichalcum* (artificial brass) in *sestertii* and *dupondii*, while the *asses* are of pure copper. For various analyses, see Mommsen-Blacas, iii. p. 38; Grueber in *Num. Chron.* 1904, p. 244.

[2] Usually these small coins (like No. 100) have been called *semisses*; but they never exceed in weight a quarter of an *as* (Grueber, *Num. Chron.* 1904, p. 241). Although weight counts for little in this token coinage, it seems more probable that they are *quadrantes*.

distinguished by their obverse types, although these were not adhered to for long. The *quadrans*, which was not struck by C. Cassius, is illustrated from a specimen bearing the names of the triumvirs Clodius Pulcher, Statilius Taurus, and Livineius Regulus, who are assigned by Ct. de Salis and Mr. Grueber to the year 13 B.C. The date of the coins of Cassius is uncertain, but they serve as well as any other to indicate the denominations introduced by Augustus when he revived the bronze coinage. There is a general agreement among numismatists in dating this revival in the year 15 B.C. Opinions differ, however, as to the year in which Augustus first allowed the monetary magistrates to place their names on the gold and silver coinage; the earliest date suggested is 20 B.C., the latest 16 B.C. For our purposes the fact of chief importance is the introduction of the new brass and copper currency. It will be noticed that, besides the names of the *triumvir a(ere) a(rgento) a(uro) f(lando) f(eriundo)*, all these new coins bear the letters S·C· (*Senatus Consulto*) in a prominent form. In other words, they record the fact that Augustus, while keeping the coinage of gold and silver in his own hands, gave to the Senate the privilege of striking the baser metals.[1] This the Senate

---

[1] For certain exceptions, in the shape of coins in these metals which, not bearing the letters S.C., appear to have been struck by imperial authority, see Strack in *Bonner Jahrbücher*, 111—112, p. 435. Cp. also F. Gnecchi, in *Riv. Ital. di Numism.*, 1908, p. 526.

HISTORICAL ROMAN COINS

retained until the middle of the third century, when the silver coinage had become so degraded that it could not, as a rule, be distinguished from copper or brass.

We are accustomed, owing to the resemblance in size between the *dupondius* and its half, the *as*, to regard the system inaugurated by Augustus as singularly unpractical. But, as we have seen, the two denominations, when fresh, were easily distinguished by their metal, with a certain amount of assistance drawn from the variation in their types. Apart from this, however, these coins were all tokens, representing an arbitrary value. The normal weight of the *sestertius* from Augustus to Elagabalus was kept, with considerable regularity, at one Roman ounce (27·29 grammes); the *dupondius* and *as* seem to have weighed the same, viz., half an ounce. The *aureus* was equivalent to 25 silver *denarii*; the *denarius* to 4 *sesterces* of brass; the *sesterce* to 4 *asses* of copper. Since the *aureus* of this period was $\frac{1}{42}$ lb., the *denarius* $\frac{1}{84}$ lb., the *sesterce* $\frac{1}{12}$ lb., and the *as* $\frac{1}{24}$ lb. in weight, we obtain the following relations between the metals, as expressed in the coinage:—

Gold to silver as 12·5 to 1.
,, brass ,, 350 ,, 1.
,, copper ,, 700 ,, 1.
Silver to brass ,, 28 ,, 1.
,, copper ,, 56 ,, 1.
Brass to ,, ,, 2 ,, 1.

HISTORICAL ROMAN COINS

In the case of the relations of the nobler to the baser metals, this could hardly have represented intrinsic value; probably the *sestertii* and smaller denominations were minted at something like double their actual value.[1]

One element of the reform of Augustus was of brief duration. The privilege which the moneyers enjoyed of placing their names on the coins was withdrawn after 3 B.C. We do not know why it was taken away, any more than we know why it was granted in the first place. It was possibly a concession to republican feeling. Although the types and legends usually have direct reference to Augustus, we have on some coins types which recall the good old days when moneyers commemorated their family history. Thus L. Aquillius Florus represents his ancestor M' Aquillius supporting Sicily, a fainting woman; another type is the three-legged symbol of Sicily. Both refer to the suppression by M' Aquillius of the slave revolt in 100 B.C. Allusions of this kind, however, are excluded from the brass and copper coinage. One may regard them as concessions made by Augustus to the moneyers working under his direct control.[2]

---

[1] On this whole question see Mommsen-Blacas, iii. pp. 42—48.

[2] Moneyers who issued gold or silver in this period very rarely issued brass or copper, and *vice versâ*. The only exceptions are M. Sanquinius and P. Licinius Stolo. It is possible, therefore, that the triumvirs were divided into two classes, one imperial, the other senatorial.

HISTORICAL ROMAN COINS

THE ALTAR OF LYON.
10 B.C.

101. *Obv.* Head of Augustus r., laureate; around, **CAESAR ΓONT MAX**.

Rev. Altar, surmounted by eight objects of uncertain significance, and decorated in front with a wreath between two small figures (?) holding laurel branches; on either side, on a column, a Victory holding a wreath and a palm branch; in exergue, **ROMETAVG**.

Bronze. 11·02 grammes (170 grains). British Museum.

102. *Obv.* Head of Augustus l., laureate; behind, caduceus.

Rev. Similar to No. 101.

Bronze. 4·40 grammes (67·9 grains). Cabinet des Médailles, Bibliothèque Nationale, Paris.

103. *Obv.* Head of Augustus r., laureate; around, **CAESAR AVGVSTVS DIVI F· ΓATER ΓATRIAE**.

Rev. Similar to preceding.

Brass. 24·76 grammes (382·2 grains). British Museum.

The great altar of Lyon was inaugurated by the Gaulish chiefs, in honour of Roma and Augustus, on 1st Aug., 10 B.C.[1] It is well known that Augustus allowed no cultus of himself alone, apart from Roma;

---

[1] See Toutain, in *Rec. des Mém. de la Soc. Nat. des Ant. de France, Centenaire*, 1904, pp. 455—459, where the date 12 B.C. is disposed of.

HISTORICAL ROMAN COINS

accordingly this altar, the focus of Romanism in Gaul, was always known as the *ara Romae et Augusti*. It was associated with the *concilium* of the Tres Galliae, sometimes called the *conventus arensis*. The *concilium* was the earliest assembly of the kind (corresponding to the Greek κοινά) to be founded in the West. It was attended at first by representatives of 60, afterwards of 64 Gaulish *civitates*.[1] The provincial priest, who presided over the *concilium*, held the title *sacerdos Romae et Augusti ad confluentes Araris et Rhodani;* and his most important function was the conduct of the festival which took place on 1st Aug., consisting of a grand procession, prayers and sacrifice for Roma and the Emperor, a banquet and athletic contests.

There can be no doubt that the erection represented on the coins Nos. 101—103 is meant for the altar, although an attempt has been made to disprove the current interpretation.[2] The wreath (*corona civica*) between the laurel branches conveys an obvious allusion to Augustus (see No. 85); the same decoration is found on the altar of the Genius Augusti at Pompeii.[3] No satisfactory explanation has, however,

[1] On the numbers, see Ferrero, *Grandezza e Decadenza di Roma*, v. p. 71. On the organization of the Tres Galliae the latest writer is Hirschfeld in *Klio*, 1908.

[2] Willers in *Numism. Zeitschr.* xxxiv. (1902) maintains that it is the *ovarium* of the circus at Lugdunum; see the reply to his article in *Rev. Numism.* 1904, pp. 46 ff. by Poncet and Morel, and in *Bonner Jahrbücher*, 111, 112, pp. 442 f. by Max L. Strack.

[3] Overbeck-Mau, *Pompeii*, 118 f.

been found for the two objects (if they are not meant for small figures) flanking the laurel branches, or for the objects on the top of the altar.

In addition to the series of coins (such as No. 101) issued at the time of the inauguration of the altar, there is a second series (to which No. 103 belongs) issued after Augustus had received the title Pater Patriae, *i.e.*, after 3 B.C. Finally, there exists a small bronze coin (No. 102) having the altar on the reverse, and a laureate head of Augustus on the obverse, with a caduceus behind it.[1] It has recently been maintained that the festival of the three Gauls was celebrated at Lugdunum on 1st Aug., because that was the date of the festival of the Gaulish Mercurius, and Augustus had been received into the Gaulish Pantheon in the character of that god. The coin seems to give some confirmation to this view.[2]

THE DEATH OF NERO DRUSUS.

9 B.C.

104. *Obv.* Head of Nero Drusus l., wearing oak wreath; around, **NERO CLAVDIVS DRVSVS GERMANICVS IMP.**

---

[1] Unfortunately much worn, so as hardly to repay reproduction.
[2] See R. Mowat, *Procès-verbaux de la Soc. Nat. des Ant. de France*, 20 Avr. 1904; the theory of Augustus and the Gaulish Mercurius is Otto Hirschfeld's (*Rec. des Mém. de la Soc. Nat. des Ant. de France, Centenaire*, 1904, pp. 211 f.).

Rev. A triumphal arch, surmounted by an equestrian statue of Drusus, charging r. with spear couched, between two trophies, each with a captive at its foot; inscription, **DE GERM**.

Aureus. 7·69 grammes (118·7 grains). British Museum.

Nero Drusus, the younger brother of Tiberius, and the favourite stepson of Augustus, died on 14th Sept., 9 B.C., as the result of a fall from his horse on his way from the Elbe to the Rhine. His body was brought to Rome, his brother Tiberius walking all the way beside the bier, and his memory was honoured in an unprecedented manner. A splendid funeral was partial compensation for the triumph of which death had robbed him. A cenotaph was erected to him on the Rhine, near Moguntiacum, and a marble triumphal arch on the Via Appia. The Senate ordered the setting up of various statues, and granted to him and to his descendants the name of Germanicus.

The triumphal arch and the name Germanicus are both recorded on the *aureus* No. 104. This coin and all the others relating to Drusus are obviously posthumous; the question is whether they were struck immediately after his death, or much later. Owing, presumably, to the fact that a coin with the portrait of Drusus was struck by his son Claudius after he became Emperor, it has been supposed that all the pieces referring to the German victories date from the reign of Claudius. It is true that some of them bear a portrait, the treatment of which recalls the style of the coins of Claudius; this is the case with the *aurei* inscribed **DE GERMANIS** in full (on a triumphal arch or around a trophy of arms). Our *aureus* with the shorter inscription, however, shows a broad treatment of the head which seems earlier, and it may well have been struck under Augustus or Tiberius.

THE SENATORIAL MINT AT ANTIOCH.
CIRCA 7—6 B.C.

105. *Obv.* Head of Augustus r., laureate; around, **ΚΑΙΣΑ[ΡΟΣ ΣΕ]ΒΑΣΤΟΥ**; fillet border.

Rev. The Tyche of Antioch, wearing turreted crown, seated r. on rock; she holds palm branch; at her feet, half-figure of the river Orontes swimming; around, **ΕΤΟΥΣ ϚΚ ΝΙΚΗΣ**, and in field, **ΥΠ** (in monogram) **ΙΒ** and monogram of **ΑΝΤΙΟΧ**.

Silver *stater*. 14·88 grammes (229·6 grains). B.M.C. *Galatia*, p. 166, No. 131.

106. *Obv.* **IMP·AVGVST· TR·POT.** Head of Augustus r., laureate; beneath head, **ΛΕ** (in monogram, retrograde).

Rev. **S·C·** within laurel wreath.

Bronze. 17·43 grammes (269 grains). B.M.C. *Galatia*, etc., p. 166, No. 128.

The policy generally adopted by the Emperors from Augustus onwards, in regard to the bronze currency of the Eastern provinces, was to leave the control in local hands. The municipal coinages sufficed for all ordinary purposes. The city of Antioch, however, was one of the three great cities of the Eastern provinces in which the Emperors established mints which played a special part in producing provincial currency. At Alexandria, the capital of the Imperial province of Egypt, the control of the coinage, both bronze and silver, remained entirely in Imperial hands; there was no municipal coinage. Augustus, in fact, simply continued the Ptolemaic system; his first Alexandrian pieces, issued in the period 30—27 B.C., are merely a continuation of the coinage of Cleopatra, with the same reverse types and the same marks of value. In a province which was peculiarly Imperial, the Senate naturally would be allowed no part in the coinage. At the mint of Caesarea in Cappadocia, which supplied the silver coinage for the greater part of Eastern Asia Minor, there is again no sign of Senatorial control. But at Antioch, the political and military centre of the Syrian province, the extensive and varied coinage falls into two or three classes. We have, first, an Imperial silver coinage (No. 105) with the portrait of Augustus, the date (calculated from the "Victory," *i.e.*, according to the Actian era, and by the Emperor's consulship[1]), and a representation of the famous figure of the Tyche of Antioch

---

[1] The abbreviation ΥΠ is for ὑπάτου.

by Eutychides of Sicyon. Again, there is a bronze coinage commemorating the assumption by Augustus of some high priesthood (whether the office of Pontifex Maximus or some local Antiochene dignity we do not know). But this coinage has a more definitely local character than the other, on which at first the name of Antioch does not appear at all. The inscriptions on these two classes are in Greek. The third class of coins with the head of Augustus is illustrated by No. 106. There is yet another small class of bronze coins, without the Emperor's head, but with the names of the legates of the province, Varus (7—4 B.C.) and Saturninus (4—5 A.D.).[1] The reverse of No. 106 tells its own tale; the coin in fact corresponds to the brass and copper coins introduced at the Roman mint by Augustus in 15 B.C. At what date, however, the Senatorial mint was established at Antioch it is difficult to determine. In 14 B.C. Augustus founded the colony of Berytus, and it might be urged that the organization of the mint at Antioch dates from the same period. But the coinage itself does not, apparently, begin until later; the first of the silver coins above mentioned is of the 26th year of the Actian era; *i.e.*, 6—5 B.C. The first coin with the name of Varus is of the preceding year, 7—6 B.C. The coins commemorating the high priesthood of

---

[1] On these various bronze issues, see Macdonald in *Numism. Chron.* 1904, pp. 105 f.

Augustus begin in 5—4 B.C., that is to say in the year when Varus's tenure of office came to an end, and some change was evidently made in the arrangements of the mint. These "archieratic" coins continued to be issued down to year 31 of the Actian era (= 1 B.C.—1 A.D.), ceasing at the same time as the silver coins with the figure of Tyche. These two issues of silver and bronze were thus, as Macdonald remarks, closely connected. As the Senatorial coinage is not likely to have been permitted before the Imperial, we may date the organization of the mint about 7—6 B.C.

There is nothing on the coin No. 106 itself to prove its attribution to the mint of Antioch. But the *provenance* of coins of this class is Syrian; and a chain of numismatic evidence, which we cannot follow here, links these coins to others which are certainly Antiochene.

GAIUS CAESAR.

CIRCA 5 B.C.

107. *Obv.* Head of Gaius Cæsar r.; below, **CAESAR**; all in oak wreath.

Rev. An incense altar, with lion's feet and ram's heads as decoration; around, a wreath containing flowers, paterae and bucrania; across field, **AVGVST**.

Aureus. 7·96 grammes (122·8 grains). B.M.C. II., p. 42, No. 4468.

This *aureus*, with the corresponding *denarius*, was assigned by Count de Salis to the mint of Rome and the year 17 B.C., in which Augustus adopted Gaius and Lucius, the sons of Agrippa by Julia. Now as Gaius was born in 734 A.U.C. = 20 B.C., he was only three years old at that time; his brother Lucius was still younger, having been born a few days before the adoption. The person whose head is represented on our coin must, however, have been at least in his teens at the time when the coin was struck; a fact which it is difficult to reconcile with the date and interpretation given to the coin by De Salis. Further, had the piece been issued to celebrate the adoption of Gaius, we should have expected to find his brother represented on the same or on an analogous coin. But this one stands alone.

It seems, therefore, that we must look somewhat later in the life of Gaius for the event which the coin commemorates. Before proceeding further, however, it is well to face any doubts we may have as to the identity of the person represented. It is just possible, but hardly probable, that the word **CAESAR** does not refer to the portrait, but is to be read with the word **AVGVST** which comes on the reverse. Even so, however, the portrait must represent some youth in intimate relationship with Augustus; and the choice lies between Gaius and Lucius. And Gaius, being the elder, is more likely to have been represented alone than his brother.

In his Will[1] Augustus says, "Gaium et Lucium

---

[1] *Mon. Anc.* ch. xiv. (Mommsen, *Res gest.*[2] pp. 51 ff.).

HISTORICAL ROMAN COINS

Caesares honoris mei caussa senatus populusque Romanus annum quintum et decimum agentis consules designavit, ut [e]um magistratum inirent post quinquennium. et ex eo die, quo deducti [s]unt in forum, ut interessent consiliis publicis decrevit sena[t]us."

The *deductio in forum* took place early in 749 = 5 B.C.[1]—perhaps, as Mommsen says, on 1st January. L. Caesar did not receive the *toga virilis* until three years later. But the designation of Gaius as consul did not necessarily take place at the same time as the *deductio in forum*.[2] Some decent interval probably elapsed. It is to this interval that we may, perhaps, without rashness, assign the coin before us. Now Dio tells us,[3] in connexion with the admission of Gaius to public affairs, that he received ἱερωσύνην τινά. In this statement we may find an explanation of our reverse type. The *thymiaterium* or incense altar and the wreath—the constituents of which are the ordinary decorations of Roman altars[4]—both indicate some priestly office, as surely as do the sacrificial implements which are so common as reverse types on Roman coins.

So far as our information goes, there is no objection to the date here suggested for this *aureus*. Placed

---

[1] Sueton. *Aug.* 26; Zonar. 10. 35 : 12th consulship of Augustus.
[2] Mommsen, *Res gest.* pp. 52 f. disposes of the current belief that Gaius was designated consul while still *praetextatus*.
[3] LV. 9.
[4] See Reisch in Pauly-Wissowa, i. 1679.

beside the coins of 17 B.C. it cannot be said that it looks "at home," even if the portrait could possibly be meant for a boy of three years. But if we bring it down to a later date, we cannot place it after the designation of Gaius as consul in 749; for such an honour would surely have been mentioned.[1] On the other hand, we can hardly put it before his assumption of the *toga virilis* early in that year, since we know of no occasion which would have justified the issue of a coin with his portrait before that event.

The fabric of the coin is somewhat peculiar, and is unlike the Roman fabric of the year to which De Salis assigned it; nor does it fit well with the Roman coins of the last ten years of the century. It is just possible that it was struck in Gaul. But if so, we are practically compelled to date it three years earlier, *i.e.*, to 8 B.C., when Gaius accompanied Tiberius on his campaign against the Sugambri. In that case, some other explanation must be found for the reverse type.

GAIUS AND LUCIUS CAESARES.

CIRCA 2 B.C.

108. *Obv.* Head of Augustus r., laureate; around, **CAESAR AVGVSTVS DIVI F · PATER PATRIAE.**

[1] *À fortiori*, the coin cannot commemorate his death, which would have been in some way alluded to.

HISTORICAL ROMAN COINS

Rev. Gaius and Lucius standing to front, each veiled and togate, holding a spear and shield; above, sacrificial ladle and lituus; in exergue, C·L·CAESARES ; around, AVGVSTIF·COS·DESIG·PRINC·IVVENT.

Aureus. 7·79 grammes (120·2 grains). British Museum.

" [Fil]ios meos, quos iuv[enes mi]hi eripuit for[tuna], Gaium et Lucium Caesares honoris mei caussa senatus populusque Romanus annum quintum et decimum agentis consules designavit, ut [e]um magistratum inirent post quinquennium . . . equites [a]utem Romani universi principem iuventutis utrumque eorum parm[is] et hastis argenteis donatum appellaverunt." [1]

Augustus received the title of *pater patriae* on Feb. 5, 2 B.C.[2] C. Caesar had already in 5 B.C. been designated consul, to enter on his consulship in the fifth ensuing year, *i.e.*, on Jan. 1, A.D. 1. This coin, therefore, since on it Augustus is called *pater patriae*, and Gaius is still consul designate, must have been struck between Feb. 5, 2 B.C. and Dec. 31, 1 B.C.

The date of the acclamation of the two adopted sons of Augustus as *principes iuventutis* is not known. Mommsen inclines to the day on which they first laid aside the *toga praetexta* and appeared in public among

---

[1] *Mon. Anc.* ch. xiv.; Mommsen, *Res gest.* pp. 51 f.
[2] *Mon. Anc.* ch. xxxv.

the equites. That is of course the most probable occasion.

The *aureus*, to judge from its inscription, seems to have been struck mainly to commemorate the honours heaped upon the two princes. L. Caesar assumed the *toga virilis* and became consul designate in 2 B.C., probably on Jan. 1.[1] It is reasonable to suppose that the coin was issued in the course of the same year. It is a brief commentary on the passages from the Monumentum Ancyranum and from Cassius Dio[2] relating to the entrance of the princes on public life. They are represented wearing the *toga virilis*; they are veiled, and sacrificial implements are placed beside them, to indicate that they held priestly offices, such as Dio mentions in connexion with Gaius. They have the silver shields and spears which the knights bestowed on them.[3]

As Mommsen has shown, the attainment of the dignity of *princeps iuventutis* was equivalent to nomination as successor to the reigning Emperor. These coins, then, must have served as a means of proclaiming the choice of Augustus. They were struck in great numbers, both in gold and silver, and circulated widely, not only in the Roman Empire, but far

---

[1] Mommsen, *Res gest.* p. 52.
[2] LIV. 18.
[3] Dio (lv. 12), in describing the funeral ceremony of Gaius and Lucius says that these decorations were dedicated in the Senate house; but he calls them golden.

beyond its limits. They are frequently found in India,[1] and it is a curious fact that the *denarii* from that source are nearly always of base metal plated with silver. Mommsen has accordingly suggested [2] that they were purposely issued for trade with South India. However this may be, the Indians found them much to their liking, and barbarous imitations continued to be made in considerable numbers for many years after the originals first appeared in India. It was not the custom of barbarians in antiquity to imitate coins of bad quality; the two Greek currencies which were most imitated by barbarians were the excellent coinages of Athens and of Philip II. of Macedon. Here we have an exception to the general rule, which awaits explanation.

THE PANNONIAN TRIUMPH OF TIBERIUS.

A.D. 13.

109. *Obv.* Head of Augustus r., laureate; around, **CAESAR AVGVST[VS] DIVI F. ΓATER ΓATRIAE.**

Rev. Tiberius in a triumphal quadriga to r., holding a sceptre surmounted by an eagle and a laurel branch; around, **TI·CAESAR AVG·F·TR·ΓOT· XV.**

Silver *denarius*. 3·16 grammes (48·7 grains). British Museum.

---

[1] See *Num. Chron.* 1898, p. 319.
[2] Mommsen-Blacas, iii. p. 337.

HISTORICAL ROMAN COINS

The dangerous Illyrico-Pannonian revolt, which broke out in A.D. 6, provoked by the demands made upon the provincials in preparation for Tiberius' expedition against the Marcomanni, was not quelled until the autumn of A.D. 9. Cassius Dio records[1] that Augustus accepted a triumph for the conclusion of this war; whether he is correct or not,[2] Tiberius at any rate was saluted imperator and granted a triumph and two triumphal arches in Pannonia. The titles "Pannonicus" and "Invictus" which it was also proposed to give him were, however, disallowed by Augustus.

The fearful disaster to the legions of Varus prevented Tiberius from immediately enjoying the honour accorded to him. He left almost at once for the Rhine, and was occupied there until the end of A.D. 12. Not until 16 Jan., A.D. 13 did he celebrate the long-delayed triumph.

The date on this *denarius* and on corresponding *aurei* (*tribunicia potestate xv.*) is equivalent to the year A.D. 13—14, and the triumph commemorated is obviously the one with which we are concerned. The event is also commemorated on the magnificent cameo at Vienna, known as the Gemma Augustea, on which Tiberius is seen alighting from his chariot to greet Augustus.[3]

---

[1] LVI. 17.
[2] See Mommsen, *Res gestae*, p. 19.
[3] Furtwängler, *Ant. Gemmen*, Taf. lvi.

HISTORICAL ROMAN COINS

This—the last "historical coin" in the present selection—has brought us well into the Imperial period. The Roman money, as we have seen (p. 121) has already borne an Imperial character for something like half a century. We stop on the threshold of an age in which the coinage is, if possible, still fuller of historical interest than we have found it during the three and a half centuries which we have surveyed.

INDEX

[*Italicised entries represent inscriptions on coins. The numbers refer to pages of the text.*]

A. C., 67, 69
Actium, victory of, 134
Ad fru. emu. ex S. C., 79
Adramytteum, Senatus consultum of, 78
Aegusa, battle of (241 B.C.), 43
Aemilia, Vestal, 121
Aemilius Lepidus, M., moneyer (65 B.C.), 52
Aemilius Lepidus, M., propraetor in Sicily (80 B.C.), 53
Aemilius Lepidus, M., tutor of Ptolemaeus V., his career, 51 ff.
Aemilius (M.), M. f. M. n. Scaurus, his campaign against Aretas, and his aedilician games, 98
Aeneas carrying Anchises, 118, 121
Aerarium populi Romani, 81, 83
Aes grave of Campania, 11, 13 ; *see also* As.
Aes rude, 14
Aes signatum, 13 f.
Africa, head of, 94 f.
Africa, Pompeius in, 94 f.
Agrippa : defeats Sex. Pompeius, 127 ; xvir sacris faciundis, 149
A. Hirtius Pr., 107
Alexandrea, 51
Alexandria : coinage of, 163 ; head of, 51; M. Antonius triumphs at, 132
Allies. *See* Social War.
Altar of Lugdunum, 158. *See also* Incense altar.
Antioch in Syria, coinage of, 162 f.
Antium, subjection of, 4
Anton, son of Hercules, 118, 121
Antoni. Armenia devicta, 132
Antoni. imp. a. xli., 124

INDEX

Antonius augur cos. des. iter. et tert., 131

Antonius, M.: portraits of, 113, 118, 120, 131 f.; his coinage as triumvir, 118; his legates in Gaul, 123 ff.; birthday coins, 124; uses lion as badge (?), 125; his relations with Ventidius, 131; his Armenian expedition, 131 ff., 147; his expedition against Phraates, 132; his triumph at Alexandria, 132; bestows kingdoms on Cleopatra and her sons, 132 f.; his cistophori, 144

Anvil, 154

Aplustre, alluding to naval victory, 122

Apollo: head of, 9, 19, 24, 72, 89, 101; "Apollo" series of aes grave, 24

Apollonia: coins issued at, 105 f.; "victoriati" of, 36

Appian Way, completion of, 10, 13, 18

Appuleius. *See* Saturninus.

Aquillius, M', coins commemorating exploits of, 157

Ara Romae et Augusti, 159

Arches. *See* Triumphal.

Aretas III., subjection of, 98 f.

Argentum Publicum, 83

Arg. Pub., 83

Ariminum, arch at, 151

Armenia: expedition of M. Antonius against, 131 ff.; given to Alexander, son of Cleopatra, 132; recovered by Augustus, 145 f.; Lesser, given to Polemo, 133 n.

Armenia devicta, 132, 134

Armenia recepta, 145

Armenian: arms, 145, 147; tiara, 131 f., 145, 147

Artavasdes, king of Armenia, 132

Artaxias, king of Armenia, 146

As: earliest libral, 6 f.; reductions in, 21 ff., 30 f., 46 f.; of Augustus, 154, 156

Asia, Commune of, organized by Augustus, 143 f.

Aug. suf. p., 148

August., 165

Augustus, 136, 138, 145

Augustus (*see also* Octavian): portraits of, 136, 138 f., 143, 145, 148, 150, 158, 162, 168, 171; receives oaken crown, laurels and golden shield, 137; recovers lost standards, 138 ff.; builds shrine for them, 141 f.; his temple of Mars Ultor, 140 f.; organizes Commune Asiae, 144 f.; celebrates secular games, 148; restores

INDEX

public roads, 150 ff. ; reforms coinage, 153 ff. ; cult of, 158 ff. ; his monetary policy in the East, 163 ; receives title of "pater patriae," 169 ; declares G. and L. Caesares his successors, 170 ; will of, *see* Monumentum Ancyranum.

Augustus tribunic. potest., 153

Augustus tr. pot. vii., 150

Aurei : of Caesar, 100 f., 104 ; of Pompeius, 94 f. ; of Sulla, 92 f. ; of the Triumvirs, 118 ff. *See also* Gold.

Ausculum, battle of (279 B.C.), 26

Axe, sacrificial, 101, 104

A. xl., a. xli., 124

BACCHANTE, head of, 85

Barbarous imitations of Roman coins, 171

Basilica Aemilia, 52 f.

Bellerophon and Pegasus, 110, 112

Bellona, head of, 7, 18

Bells on column of Augurinus, 64

Beneventum : battle of, 26 ; mint of, 46

Biga : of Luna, 56 ; of Victory, 56, 82

Bigati, 60

Bocchus surrenders Jugurtha, 70 f.

Brass coinage of Augustus, 154

"Bricks," quadrilateral, issued by Roman mint, 11, 14 ff., 26

Bronze : its relation to silver, 5, 12, 17, 21 f., 29 ff., 48 ; ceremonia use of, 15 ; cessation of coinage in, 90. *See also* Aes.

Brundusium, colony of, 31

Brut. imp., 116

Bruttian silver coinage, 35

Brutus imp., 116

Brutus (Q. Caepio), the tyrannicide, in Asia and Macedon, 116 f ; portrait, 116

Bull goring wolf, 85, 87

Buteo, 84

Caesar, 101, 165

Caesar Augustus, 186, 189

Caesar Augustus Divi f. Pater Patriae, 158, 168, 171

Caesar Augustus tribunic. potest., 154

Caesar Augustus tr. pot., 148

INDEX

Caesar (C. Iulius): portrait of, 110, 112, 120; increases military stipendium, 49; returns to Rome (49 B.C.), 100 f.; his fourfold triumph, 107 ff.; founds Corinth, 110; murdered, 112 f.
Caesar cos. vii. civibus servateis, 136
Caesar Dict. perpetuo, 112
Caesar Divi f., 134
Caesar pont. max., 158
Caesarea in Cappadocia, coinage of, 163
Caesares, Gaius et Lucius, 165 ff.
Caldus. *See* Coelius.
Caldus IIIvir, 76
Calendar, reformed in 191 B.C., 59
Caleno, 9
Calpurnius Piso, C., establishes Ludi Apollinares, 92
Calpurnius Piso Caesoninus, L., coin of, 79, 81
Calpurnius Piso Frugi, L., coinage of, 91
Campania: relations with Rome in 4th cent., 4, 5; Romanization of, 10 ff.
Campanian: didrachm, 5, 9; drachm superseded by victoriatus, 36
Canting allusions, 61, 63
Canusium, mint of, 46
Cap of Liberty, 116 f.
Capitol, Roman mint on, 8
Capua: mint at, 9, 24 f., 35; Hannibal's coinage in, 50. *See also* Campania.
Carthaginians: relations with Rome in 4th cent., 4, 7 ff.; influence on Roman coinage, 9, 13
Casca Longus, 116
Casca Longus (P. or C. Servilius), coin of, 117
Cassei, 123
Cassius, C., at Rhodes (48 B.C.), 121 f.
Cassius Longinus, C., coin of, 69
Cassius Longinus, L., moneyer about 52 B.C., 69
Cassius Longinus, Q. (quaestor 54 B.C.), coin of, 69
Cassius Longinus Ravilla, L., his judicial reforms, etc., 69 f.
Caudine Forks, 87
C. Aug., 62
C. Caesar cos. ter., 107
C. Caesar IIIvir r. p. c., 118
C. Caldus Imp. A. X., 76

INDEX

C. Cassei imp., 121
C. Cassi, 67
C. Cassius Celer iiivir a.a.a.f.f., 153
C. Cassius C. f. Celer iiivir. a.a.a.f.f., 153
C. Coel. Caldus Cos., 75
C. Coponius Pr., 101
C. Egnatulei. C. f., 72
C. Fabi. C. f., 82
Chariot. See Biga, Quadriga.
C. Hypsaeus Cos., 98
Cimbri, 73 f.
Circensian games, 115
Cista : for voting, see Voting-box ; mystica, 86
Cistophori, 143 f.
Citizen : appealing, 67 ; voting, 68
Civib. et sign. milit. a Part. recup., 139, 153
Civibus servateis, 136
Claudius Caecus, Ap., the Censor, 18
Claudius Marcellus, C., cos. 49 B.C., 105
C. L. Caesares Augusti f. cos. desig. princ. iuvent., 169
Clementia Caesaris, temple of, 113 f.
Cleopatra : portrait of, 182 f. ; gifts of M. Antonius to, ibid.
Cleopatrae reginae regum filiorum regum, 132
Clodius, P., M. f., moneyer, 119
Clodius Pulcher, moneyer, 155
Cloulius, T., coin of, 72 f.
Clovius, C., praefect, 108
Club and lion-skin with bow and arrow, 101
Clupeus virtutis, 137
Coelius Caldus, C., founder of the family, his career, 75 f.
Coelius Caldus, C., Imp., Augur, xvir sacris faciundis, 78
Coelius Caldus, C., moneyer, 76
Coelius Caldus, L., epulo, 78
Column of L. Minucius Augurinus, 62 ff.
Com. Asiae, 143
Conventus arensis, 159
Coponius, C., coin of, 101
Copper coinage of Augustus, 154
Corcyra, Roman mint at, 36, 44 ff.
Corinth refounded, 110 f.

INDEX

Corinthian coinage in the West, 14
Corinthum, 110
Cornelius Sulla, Faustus, coin of, 71. *See also* Sulla.
Corn-laws, 79 f.
Corn-supply of Rome, 63, 79 f.
Cornucopiae, 154
Cos, victory of Cassius near, 123
C. Paapi. C., 85
Crab, badge of Cos, 122
Crassus defeated by Parthians, 140
Croton, Roman mint at, 35 f.
Cupid on coin of Sulla, 92

DAGGERS and cap of Liberty, 116 f.
Dalmatians, standards recovered from, 140
Debts, remission of, 23
Decidius Saxa, L., defeated by Parthians, 140
Decimal division of the as, 21 f.
Deductio in forum, 167
De Germ., 161
De Germanis, 162
Delphi, dedication by Flamininus at, 66
Denarius: introduction of, 28 ; equated to 16 asses, 47 ff. ; reduced, 48
Desultor, 115
Diana: confused with Luna, 58 ; bust of, 70 f.
Dionysiac types on coins of Social War, 88
Dioscuri, 9, 27, 28, 33, 38, 46, 65, 85
Drusus. *See* Nero Drusus.
Duoviri of Corinth, 111 f.
Dupondius of Augustus, 153 f., 156
Dyrrhachium : "victoriati " of, 36 ; coins issued at, 105

EAGLE : holding thunderbolt, 10, 14 ; standing on thunderbolt, 37 f. ; as symbol of sovereignty, 136, 138
Egnatuleius, C., coin of, 72 f.
Egypt. *See* Alexandria, Ptolemaeus.
Eid. Mar., 116
Electrum coinage, 50 f.
Elephant, 19, 26

INDEX

E. L. P., 89, 91
Epulo, 76, 78
Ἔτους sκ' Νίκης, 162
Ewer, sacrificial, 92 f., 94
Ex A. Pu., 82 f.
Ex S. C., 81, 98, 126 f.

FABIUS, C., coin of, 82, 84
Fabius Maximus, Q., dictator, 47 f.
Faustulus the shepherd, 57, 61
Faustus, 70
Felix, 70
Fig-tree, ruminal, 57, 61
Fiscus, 116
Flamen's apex, 65
Flaminian Way, 151
Flamininus. *See* Quinctius.
Frugi, 89
Fufius Calenus, governor in Gaul, 124
Fulvia, wife of M. Antonius, portrait of, 125

GAIUS CAESAR, coins relating to, 165 ff.; his career, 166 f.
Galley in harbour of Messana, 126. *See also* Prow.
Gaul: legates of M. Antonius in, 123 f.; worship of Rome and Augustus in, 159
Gaulish trophy, 101, 103
Gemma Augustea, 172
General with lictor and citizen, 67
Germanicus, title given to Nero Drusus, 161
Gold coins: first issued at Capuan mint, 25; attributed to 242 B.C., 37 ff.; issued in times of stress, 39, 42; issued by the Allies, 86; becomes part of ordinary Roman currency, 120; relation to silver, 156. *See also* Aurei.

HANNIBALIAN crisis, 39 ff., 46 ff.
Hatria, Roman mint at, 35
Hercules, head of, 1, 7, 9
Herdonea, mint of, 46
Hirtius, A., 108
His., 76
Horse: 9, 89, 128; Parthian, 128, 130; head of, 1, 9

181

INDEX

Horseman (desultor), 113, 115
HS, see IIS
Hybreas the orator, 129
Hypsaeus. *See* Plautius.

IEIUS, MINIUS, coin of, 81
IIIvir a.a.a.f.f., 154
IIIvir r.p.c., 124
IIS, 27, 29
Illyrico-Pannonian revolt, 172
Imp. August. tr. pot., 162
Imp. Caesar, 134
Imp. Caesar. tr. pot. iix., 148
Imp. Caes. Aug. Lud. Saec., 148
Imperator, Octavian's use of title, 135 f.
Imperial coinage, origins of, 102, 121
Imper. iterum, 92
Imperium, military, 68
Imp. ix. tr. po. v., 143
Imp. tertio IIIvir r.p.c., 131
Incense altar, 165, 167
India, Roman coins from, 171
Italia, 85
Italia (Corfinium), 87
Italia, head of, 85 ff.

JANIFORM head of Persephone, 50
Janus, head of, 1, 7, 18 f., 25
Janus-Mercurius series, 24
Jugurtha, surrender of, 70 f.
Juno Moneta, 7 f.
Jupiter: on coins of Lentulus and Marcellus, 107; in quadriga, 19, 50; head of, 7, 44, 46; Feretrius, temple of, 141 f.

Καίσαρος Σεβαστοῦ, 162
Karnyx, 72, 78
Keltic arms on trophies, etc., 73, 76 f.

LABIENUS, Q., career and coinage of, 128 ff.
Laeca, 66
Largess, coins struck for, 109. *See also* Triumphs.

INDEX

Latin League reorganised (358 B.C.), 4
Laurel-branches, bestowed on Augustus, 136 f.
Laus Iuli. Corint., 110
L. *Caldus VIIvir epul.*, 76
L. *Certo Aeficio C. Iulio IIvir.*, 110.
L. D., 75
Lectisternium, 76 f.
Leges: Acilia (191 B.C.), 59 ; annalis, 103 ; Appuleia frumentaria de semissibus et trientibus, 79 ; Cassia tabellaria, 69 ; Clodia (104 B.C.), 37, 72 ; Coelia tabellaria, 77 ; Flaminia minus solvendi, 47 ; Iulia Papiria, 2 ; Ogulnia, 63 ; Papiria de asse semunciali, 89 f. ; Plautia Papiria, 90 ; Porciae, 68 ; Tarpeia, 2
Leg. xvi., 125
Lent. Mar. Cos., 105
Lentulus Crus, L., cos. 49 B.C., 105
Lepidus. *See* Aemilius.
Libella, 22, 25
Liberty : in quadriga, 66 ff. ; head of, 116, 121 ; cap of, 116 f.
Lictor attending general, 67
Lion: used by M. Antonius as a badge (?), 124 f. ; head of, on column of Augurinus, 64
Lituus, 62, 70 f., 92 f., 94, 107, 126, 128, 169
Livineius Regulus, moneyer (c. 13 B.C.), 155
Livineius Regulus, L., moneyer (43—38 B.C.), 119
L. Lent. C. Marc. Cos., 104
L. Mescinius, 148
L. Mescinius Rufus IIIvir, 148
Local Roman coinage of Italy, 35 f., 40, 46, 68
Longin. IIIV., 68
L. P. D. A. P., 89, 91
L. Plaet. Cest., 116
L. Regulus IIIIvir a.p.f., 118
L. Sauf., 56
L. Sesti. proq., 116
L. Sulla, 92
Luceria, Roman mint at, 35 f., 46
Lucilius Rufus, M., 82
Lucius Caesar, coin representing, 168 f.
Lucullus, coinage of, 92 f.
Ludi Apollinares, 92

INDEX

Lud. S., 148
Lugdunum: coins struck at, 124 f., 158 f.; altar of, 158 ff.
Luguduni, 124
Luna: in biga, 56 ff.; worship of, 58; reason for appearance on coinage, 59.
L. Vinicius L. f. iiivir, 150
Lyon. *See* Lugdunum.

MACEDONIAN shield, symbol of Macedonian victory, 65
Magna Mater, head of, 82, 84
Magnesia, battle of, 60
Magnus, 94
Mag. Pius. imp. iter., 126
M. Antonius IIIvir r.p.c., 72
Marcellus. *See* Claudius.
Marius defeats the Barbarians, 72 f.
Mars: holding standards, 139; within temple, *ib.*; head of, 1, 37 f.; Ultor, 139 ff., 151 f.
Mar. Ult., 139
Massalia, 3-scruple drachms of, 37
Mercurius: Gaulish, Augustus identified with, 160; Roman, head of, 7, 18 f., 27.
Mescinius Rufus, coins of, 148
Messana, pharos of, 126, 128
Mi. Ieuis. Mi., 86
Military coinage, 101 f.
Minerva, head of, 7, 89
Minucius Augurinus, C., 62 ff.
Minucius Augurinus, L., 62 ff.
Minucius Augurinus, P., 63
Minucius Augurinus, Ti., 65
Minucius Faesus, M., 62 f.
Mithradates and the Allies, 86 ff.
M. Lepidus An. XV. Pr. H. O. C. S., 52
M. Lepidus IIIvir r.p.c., 118
M. Lepidus Tutor Regis Pontif. Max., 51 f.
M. Lucili. Ruf., 82
Moneta, supposed origin of the name, 8
Moneyers: gradual appearance of their marks, etc., on coinage, 61 f.; under Augustus, 120, 157. *See also* Tresviri, Quattuorviri.

INDEX

Monumentum Ancyranum (will of Augustus), 136 f., 140, 146, 149, 151, 166 f., 169
Moon-goddess. *See* Luna.
M. Porc., 66
M. Scaur. aed. cur., 98
M. Servilius leg., 122
Mulvian bridge, arch on, 152
Mussidius Longus, L., moneyer, 119
Mutil. embratur, 85
Mutilus. *See* Papius.

NABATHAEA. *See* Aretas III.
Neapolis, silver coinage of, 35
Neptune: Octavian represented as, 135; statue of, on pharos of Messana, 128
Nero Claudius Drusus Germanicus imp., 160
Nero Drusus, death of, 160

OAK-WREATH: bestowed on Augustus, 136 f., 153; worn by Venus (?), 102
Oath-taking scene, 19, 25, 85, 87 f.
Ob civis servatos, 153
Octavian: portraits of, 118; as triumvir (43—38 B.C.), 118; growth of his power reflected in coinage, 120; his triumph in 29 B.C., 134 f.; receives title "Augustus," 135 ff.; represented as Neptune, 135; use of title "imperator," 135 f. *See* Augustus.
Oppius Statianus defeated by Parthians, 140
Orontes, river, 162
Osco-Latin standard, 5
Ox as coin-type, 3

PACORUS of Parthia invades Syria, 129
Paestum, late bronze coinage of, 91
Pannonian triumph of Tiberius, 171 f.
Papirius Carbo, C., his lex de asse semunc., 89 f.
Papius, C., Mutilus, coins of, 85 ff.
Parthians: joined by Labienus, 129 f.; restore the standards, 139 ff.
Parthicus, title taken by Q. Labienus, 128 f.
Pater patriae, title of Augustus, 169
Pecunia, origin of name, 2
Pegasus, 11, 14. *See also* Bellerophon.

185

INDEX

Pergamum: coins struck at, 142, 145, 147; temple of Rome and Augustus at, 145
Persephone, janiform head of, 50
Personal names and types on coins of Republic, 60; of Augustus, 157
Phraates IV. of Parthia: M. Antonius attacks, 132; restores standards, 139 f.
Phrygian helmet worn by Roma, 13
P. Hypsaeus aed. cur., 98
Picus Martis, 61
Pietas, head of, 102, 109
Piso, 89
Piso Caepio Q., 45
P. Laeca, 66
Plaetorius (L.) Cestianus, moneyer, 117
Plated coins, 171
Plautius, Hypsaeus (or Decianus), C., 100
Plautius Hypsaeus, P., curule aedile, coin of, 99
Pliny: on earliest Roman coinage, 2 f.; on introduction of the denarius, 28 f.; on reduction of the as, 31 f., 47; on earliest gold coinage, 38 ff.; on equation of denarius to 16 asses, 47; on victoriatus, 72 f.
Pompaedius Silo, Q., coin of, 85 ff.
Pompeius, Cn., Cn. f., 97, 126
Pom(peius ?) Fostlus, Sex., denarius of, 57 ff.
Pompeius Magnus, Cn.: his African campaign, 94 f.; sends Scaurus against Aretas III., 99; sends Lentulus and Marcellus to Epirus, 105; portrait of, 126
Pompeius, Sextus, Cn. f., his career, 126 f.
Pompeius, Sextus (first cousin once removed of the IIIvir), 98
Portraits of living persons on coins, 114, 120
Poseidon of Corinth, 110
Pound: of 273 grammes, 6; of 327·45 grammes, 6, 24 f.; of 341 grammes, 24
Pr. = Praetor or Praefectus, 108
Praef. clas. et orae marit. ex S. C., 126
Praefecti of the City appointed by Caesar, 46 B.C., 108
Praetors appointed by Caesar, 46 B.C., 108
Preiver. Captu., 98
Priestly office, symbols of, 93, 107, 116, 170
Princeps iuventutis, meaning of title, 170

INDEX

Prisoner tied to trophy, 101
Privernum captured, 100
Pro cos., 94
Provincial cult of Rome and Augustus, 144 f.
Provocatio, 68
Provoco, 67
Prow of galley: 1, 6, 13, 18, 27, 89; as mint-mark on coin of M. Antonius and Cleopatra, 134; Victory on, 134 f.
P. *Sepullius Macer*, 113
P. *Tadi Chilo C. Iuli. Nicep. IIvir.*, 110
Ptolemaeus IV. and the Romans, 53
Ptolemaeus V. and M. Aemilius Lepidus, 51 ff.
Pu., 82 f.
Pulcher, Clodius, moneyer, 155
Pulcher Taurus Regulus, 154
Punic War, First, 37 ff.
Purgamenta, 149
Pydna, battle of, 60
Pyrrhus, war with, 20, 26

Q = quaestor, 105, 116, 118
Q = quinarius, 49, 72, 74
Q. *Caepio Brutus procos.*, 116
Q. *Cassius*, 67
Q. *Labienus Parthicus imp.*, 128
Q. *Sicinius IIIvir*, 101
Q. *Silo*, 85
Quadrans, 7, 154
Quadriga: of Jupiter, 50, 98, 100; of Liberty, 66 ff.; triumphal, 94 f., 134, 171
Quadrigatus, 19, 25, 35
Quattuorviri auro publico feriundo, 119
Quinarius, 29, 72 f., 123 ff.
Quinctius Flamininus, T., moneyer, 65
Quinctius Flamininus, T., victor of Cynoscephalae, 65 f.
Quindecimviri sacris faciundis, 148
Quod viae mun. sunt, 150

REDUCTION: of the as, 22, 46 f.; of the denarius, 48
Regulus. *See* Livineius.

INDEX

Rex Aretas, 98
Rhodes plundered by Cassius, 122
Roads, public, 150 f. *See also* Appian Way.
Roma, 12, 18, 19, 27, 28, 37, 38, 44, 46, 56, 57; disappears from the coins, 56
Roma, the goddess: head of, 10, 18, 27, 33, 38, 46, 56 f., 62, 65 ff., 82; temple of, 143 f., 145, 147; worship of, 143 ff., 158 ff.
Romano, 1, 9, 10, 12, 17
Romanom, 11, 12
Rom. et Aug., 158
Rom. et August., 143
Romulus and Remus. *See* Wolf and Twins.

S., 7, 27
Sacrificial instruments, 92 f., 107, 116, 170
Samnites: in 4th cent., 4; in 3rd cent., 19
Sanquinius, M., coins of, 149
Saturn, head of, 79
Saturninus (L. Appuleius), corn-law of, 79 f.
Saturninus, legate in Syria, 164
Saufeius, L., denarius of, 56 ff.
S.C., 83, 101 f., 121, 136, 153 ff., 162
Scaurus. *See* Aemilius.
Scruple, 17
Scylla, 126, 128
Secession of the plebs (288—286 B.C.), 23
Secular games, 148 f.
Semi-libral as, 22
Semis, 7
Sempronius Gracchus, Ti., moneyer, 37 B.C., 120
Semuncial standard, 89 f.
Senate, its control of coinage, 121, 155, 162 f.
Senatorial Party exiled from Rome, 104 f.
Sepullius (P.) Macer, coins of, 113
Series marks on coins, 75
Serrati, 60, 84
Servilius Caepio, Q., coin of, 79
Servilius, M., legate of Cassius, 123
Servius, King, 2.
Sestertius, 29; of Augustus, 153 f., 156

INDEX

Sestius, L., coin of, 117
Sex. Pom. Fostlus, 57
Sextans, 7
Sextantal standard, 30 f., 43
Shield of valour bestowed on Augustus, 136 f.
Sicily: coins of Lentulus and Marcellus connected with, 106 ; Sex. Pompeius in, 126 ff.
Sicinius, Q., coin of, 101
Sickle of Saturn, 79, 81
Signis Parthicis receptis, 138
Signis receptis, 139
Silo. *See* Pompaedius.
Silver: restriction of local coinage in, 135 ; relation to brass and copper, 156 ; relation to bronze, 5, 12, 17, 21 f., 29 ff., 48
Sitella. *See* Voting urn.
Social War, 82—89
Sol, head of, 76 f.
Soldiers: clasping hands, 86 ; pay of, 48 f. ; taking oath. *See* Oath-taking.
Sorticula. *See* Voting tablet.
Sow, 19
Spain, Pompeius in, 96
Spanish boar-standard, 77
S.P.Q.R. Cl. V., 136
S.P.Q.R. Imp. Cae. quod v. m. s. ex ea p. q. is ad a. de., 150
S. P. Q. R. Imp. Caesari, 150
S. P. Q. R. Imp. Caesari Aug. cos. xii. tr. pot. vi., 139
Standards, military : recovered by Augustus, 138 ff. ; boar-shaped, 76 f.
Statilius Taurus, moneyer, 155
Stipendium of Roman soldier, 48 f.
Struck bronze, introduction of, 23
Subsellium, 116
Suesano, 10
Suffimenta, 149
Sulla : receives Jugurtha from Bocchus, 70 f. ; disembarks at Brundusium, 87 ; in Greece, 92 f. ; acknowledges Pompeius as Magnus, 95 ; his triumphal coins, 97. *See also* Cornelius.
Swine and elephants, 26
Symbols on coinage, a mark of lateness, 40, 43
Syria, coins issued in, 130

INDEX

TARENTUM: relations with Rome in the 3rd. cent., 20; late silver coinage 35, 37
Taurus, moneyer, 155
T. Clouli., 72
Temple: of Mars Ultor, 139 ff. ; of Rome and Augustus, 143
Teutons, 73 f.
Thymiaterium, 167
Thyrsos, as ornament of galley, 128
Tiberius: occupies Armenia, 146 f.; brings body of Nero Drusus to Rome, 161 ; his Pannonian triumph, 171 f.
Ti. Caesar Aug. f. tr. pot. xv., 171
Tigranes, son of Artavasdes, king of Armenia, 146
Token money, 9, 22, 90
T. Q., 65
Trasimene, crisis after, 39, 46 ff.
Tresviri A. A. A. F. F., 82
Tresviri monetales, 62
Triens, 7
Triental standard, 30
Triskeles symbol of Sicily, 106
Triumphal arches: of Augustus, 139 f., 150 ff. ; of Nero Drusus, 161 ; of Tiberius, 172
Triumphs, coins relating to, 95 ff., 134, 171
Triumvirate: of 43—38 B.C., 118 f. ; monetary. *See* Tresviri.
Trophies, 72, 76, 92 f., 101, 103, 116. *See also* Victory.
Tyche of Antioch, 162 f.

UNCIA, 7
Uncial standard, 46
Urban coinage, 102

V., 27, 29
Varus, legate in Syria, 164
Veiled head: of Caesar, 115 ; of Liberty, 116; of Pietas, 107, 109
Ventidius Bassus, P.: governor in Gaul, 124 ; crushes Labienus, 130 181 ; his service under Antonius, 131
Venus: head of, 92, 102 f. ; Victrix, 113, 115
Vercingetorix, 103
Vest., 67
Vesta: head of, 67 ; temple of, 67 ff.

INDEX

Vestal virgins, 69, 121
Veturius, Ti., coin of, 88
Vibius Varus, C., moneyer, 119
Vibo Valentia, Roman mint at, 36, 46
Vicarello, deposit of, 16, 24
Victoriatus: origin of, 35 f., 44 ff. ; struck at Corcyra, 44 ff. ; revived by lex Clodia, 72 f.
Victory: crowning Liberty, 66 ; crowning trophy, 28, 44, 46, 72 ; driving chariot, 50, 56, 82 ; fastening taenia to palm branch, 10 ; flying, before shield of Valour, 136 ff. ; Fulvia as, 125 ; standing on prow, 134 f. ; statue of, in Senate House, 137 ; writing on shield, 72
Virga viatoris, 116
Voconius Vitulus, Q., moneyer, 120
Voting: box, 70 ; tablets, 67 ff., 75, 77 ; urn, 67 ff.

WHEEL, 10, 12 f.
Wolf: gored by bull, 85, 87 ; suckling twins, 9, 57

X as mark of value, 49
✵ as mark of value, 49
XVI as mark of value, 49
XV. S. F., 148

ZEUS ELEUTHERIOS, statue of, 107

| || (= 52), 100, 103
↓X (= 60), 37

PL. I

Nos. 1—3.

PL. II

Nos. 4, 5.

No. 6 (OBVERSE).

PL. IV

No. 6 (REVERSE).

PL. V

Nos. 7, 8.

PL. VI

Nos. 9—11.

PL. VII

No. 12 (OBVERSE).

PL. VIII

No. 12 (REVERSE).

PL. IX

Nos. 13—27.

PL. X

Nos. 28—45.

Nos. 46—60.

PL. XII

Nos. 61—74.

PL. XIII

Nos. 75—88.

PL. XIV

Nos. 89—100.

PL. XV

Nos. 101—109.